Contents

FIXER-UPPER

How to Repair America's Broken Housing Systems

JENNY SCHUETZ

BROOKINGS INSTITUTION PRESS
Washington, D.C.

Copyright © 2022 by Jenny Schuetz
THE BROOKINGS INSTITUTION
1775 Massachusetts Avenue, N.W.
Washington, D.C. 20036
www.brookings.edu

The Brookings Institution is a private nonprofit organization devoted to research, education, and publication on important issues of domestic and foreign policy. Its principal purpose is to bring the highest quality independent research and analysis to bear on current and emerging policy problems. Interpretations or conclusions in Brookings publications should be understood to be solely those of the authors.

Library of Congress Control Number: 2021951983

ISBN 9780815739289 (paperback)
ISBN 9780815739296 (ebook)

9 8 7 6 5 4 3 2 1

Typeset in Kepler Std

Composition by Elliott Beard

Acknowledgments

My dissertation adviser, Tony Gómez-Ibáñez, told me that writing a book is qualitatively different from writing journal articles: it forces you to engage with larger-scale ideas over a longer narrative arc. He was right (as usual). Some of the ideas in this book I have been mulling over in my head for many years, but putting them down on paper in semicoherent form has pushed me to think more deeply, more critically, and more concretely—even about topics I thought I already understood. Researching and writing the book have been terrific learning exercises for me; I hope that readers will also come across ideas that push them outside their comfort zones.

Many friends and colleagues have helped nudge the book into existence. Chris Redfearn deserves special thanks (or blame) for casually asking me at the AREUEA conference in San Diego: "So when are you going to write a book?" Cross-country flights provide quiet thinking space that is conducive to writing chapter outlines, as it turns out. My students in Georgetown's urban planning program have been an excellent sounding board for much of this material, tucked into lecture notes, and have helped me learn how to present complicated economic concepts with as little jargon as possible. Lyndsey Blessing kindly shared her expert knowledge on how book publishing works. I am enormously grateful for colleagues who took time away from their own work to offer thoughtful suggestions, corrections, and healthy skepticism on early chapter drafts: Adie Tomer, Anna Tranfaglia, Emily Badger, Jackie Begley, Jeff Larrimore, Pam Blumenthal, Patrick Chuang, and Tracy Gordon. Thanks also to two anonymous reviewers who provided insightful, constructive, and (uncharacteristically for economists) encouraging comments. All remaining errors and omissions—and certainly all the policy recommendations—are entirely my own.

My colleagues at Brookings have supported me throughout the project, especially Alan Berube, Amy Liu, Andre Perry, David Lanham, and Richard Reeves, as well as Bill Finan and the team at the Brookings Institution Press. Cecile Murray coauthored several of the blog posts and briefs that evolved into chapters. Sarah Crump provided excellent support with fact-checking, graphics, and general research assistance.

Writing the book would not have been possible without the love and support of my family. My parents, Verna and Arnold Schuetz, cheered me on and kept me updated on the local housing debates in Blacksburg, Virginia. My deepest, most heartfelt thanks go to my husband, Joe Sill, for his (nearly) endless patience, encouragement, and practical and moral support. On our daily walks, Joe and our dog Trooper have heard more grumbling about unreasonable zoning and inefficient land use than they ever anticipated. Every day I write the book, every day you tell me that I can.

1

Housing Sits at the Intersection
of Several Complex Systems

Between 2007 and 2009, millions of American homeowners lost their homes in an unprecedented wave of foreclosures that precipitated the United States—and the world—into the Great Recession. The aftermath of the foreclosure crisis was devastating, not just for borrowers who defaulted, but for neighbors whose homes lost value, and for entire communities.[1] The precipitous drop in property values led many homeowners to reduce their spending, which in turn hurt local economies.[2] The ripple effects that unfolded during the Great Recession demonstrated the complex series of connections between housing markets and other sectors of the economy. A decade later, alarm bells rang again as the COVID-19 pandemic disrupted the economy and threatened the stability of millions of renters.[3]

During the years after the foreclosure crisis, housing fell off the national policy stage. Most middle- and upper-income U.S. households enjoy excellent housing outcomes, compared to historical and global standards. They live in homes that are in good physical condition with ample space. Amenities like air-conditioning and spare bedrooms are taken for granted. Out-of-pocket housing costs don't unduly strain the monthly budgets of middle-class homeowners, and the equity in their homes provides a financial cushion for rainy days. Housing systems work well for these families—as they were designed to.

And yet, the nation's growing divides—by geography, income, race, and age—are reflected in and exacerbated by inequalities in housing markets. Even before the COVID-19 pandemic, more than 10 million renter households spent over half their income on rent.[4] Low-income Americans struggle to afford decent-quality housing in safe neighborhoods. Black and Latino families still face high barriers to becoming homeowners, due to persistent discrimination. Every year, millions of homes are destroyed and families displaced as a result of wildfires, flooding, intense storms, and other climate-related disasters. Where people live is increasingly correlated with important life outcomes, from school performance to employment to life expectancy. A family earning the national median income (about $68,000 in 2020) can afford to buy a good-condition, three-bedroom home in the suburbs of Dallas or Cleveland for monthly payments that would barely cover rent on a studio apartment in the San Francisco Bay Area. Millennials lag previous generations in buying homes, and have substantially less housing wealth than their parents or grandparents at their age.

These discrepancies in housing well-being by place and population characteristics help explain why housing has drawn little attention in national policy debates. Politically, it is hard to convince a majority of voters to support large-scale policy changes when millions of middle-class Americans are financially invested in the current system.

This book explores the key structural problems within U.S. housing systems that contribute to widely disparate outcomes. Many of the persistent problems are rooted in outdated laws and regulations, including decades of institutional discrimination against Black people. Policies that govern seemingly different parts of our economy—from local school funding to federal transportation policy—interact to reinforce bad housing outcomes. Throughout the book, I identify gaps between how economists believe markets ought to work and how our housing systems work in practice. For each structural problem, I propose a set of policy changes that would improve housing outcomes for individuals and communities.

A patchwork of federal, state, and local policies impacts housing markets

Stable, decent-quality housing is critical to individual and community well-being. Many of us who have the good fortune to live in comfortable, stable homes take for granted how much that impacts our daily lives. A home does more than offer physical protection from the elements and space to store our belongings. At its best, a home provides a peaceful, private place to return to after work or school, to host family and friends for holidays and other celebrations. Homes are located in neighborhoods, offering connections to a community of nearby people. Owning one's home can help build a nest egg, providing financial security for the future.

But for millions of Americans, being well housed is more of an aspiration than a reality. Widespread housing insecurity results from policy choices made not just by our elected officials and anonymous bureaucrats but by ordinary citizens showing up at neighborhood meetings.

The United States doesn't have one comprehensive housing policy. Rather, we have a complex network of rules and regulations, taxes and subsidies, formal procedures and informal social practices, all of which influence housing outcomes. We need to better integrate and coordinate a range of related policies—transportation, infrastructure funding, wealth-building—with direct housing policies like mortgage markets and rental subsidies.

The U.S. housing system is and will continue to be largely oriented around private markets. Most Americans live in housing that was financed and built with private resources, by for-profit companies. Two-thirds of American households own their own home. Even among renters,

90 percent live in privately owned housing—social housing is much less common here than in other developed countries.[5] This is not to say that public policies aren't important—they define the rules under which markets operate—but government's role is often behind the scenes.

In many ways, housing policies in the United States upend the way markets are supposed to work. Local governments tightly regulate the production of new housing, especially for lower-cost homes. Through the federal tax system, the United States heavily subsidizes demand for housing, with the largest subsidies accruing to the wealthiest families. Ask economists what happens when we limit supply and boost demand for a particular good, and they will predict that prices of that good will increase—a prediction supported by several decades of housing market data. (As we shall see throughout the book, housing markets are much more complicated than the models taught in a typical Econ 101 class, but fundamental dynamics of supply and demand still apply.)

What does a well-functioning housing system look like?

To judge whether housing policies are successful, we first need to define clear objectives, benchmarks against which to compare measurable outcomes. A well-functioning housing system should meet the following criteria:

- Housing supply should be reasonably responsive to demand. This implies that national and regional housing markets should produce enough additional housing to meet increases in demand, as driven by population and job growth.

- Within a city or metropolitan area, some new housing should be added in the neighborhoods with highest demand, where people most want to live. (This doesn't imply that the most in-demand neighborhoods can accommodate everyone who wants to live there.)

- Markets should provide a diverse set of housing choices that match household budgets and preferences.

- Regardless of income, all people can afford decent quality, stable housing in healthy communities. Chapter 4 discusses clear economic and social benefits for neighborhoods, cities, and regions that have a well-housed population.

Compared to many consumer goods and services, housing has some unusual characteristics that can create market frictions and make it difficult to achieve these outcomes. First, housing supply adjusts slowly over time. Developing a new subdivision or apartment building takes time. Unlike most consumer goods, home builders can't quickly ramp up production to meet a rapid increase in the demand for homes. The durability of homes creates even more stickiness when demand declines: homes don't magically disappear when they are no longer needed. Cities or neighborhoods that have lost population often have high vacancy rates.[6] Demand can be sticky too, because of the costs involved with moving. Most people don't upgrade to a fancier home every time they get a promotion, or downsize immediately after their children move away.

Second, housing demand and supply are deeply rooted in place. People choose where to live based on the location of their job, their family and friends, and amenities like school quality and weather. Increasing demand for homes in California can't be satisfied by building more homes in Oklahoma. (Even with prefabricated modular housing, the host city has to provide land and infrastructure.) People can and do move away from places where housing supply is tight and prices are high—and places where housing is cheap but jobs are scarce—but moving has high financial, professional, and personal costs.[7]

Third, and most important, all changes to housing supply require explicit approval from local governments. Ford and General Motors don't have to ask government permission to increase the number of cars or SUVs that their factories produce. But it is illegal for landowners and home builders to construct a single new home without the approval of the city or county in which the land is located. Even changes to existing buildings, like tearing down an empty house or converting a garage into an apartment, requires local government permission. City councils often have political reasons for limiting new housing development, especially if their constituents resist changes to their neighborhoods. Chapter 2 discusses the complex set of regulations around new development that often inhibits housing supply from adjusting to changes in demand.

Getting to better housing outcomes isn't just a question of maximizing economic efficiency. Housing and neighborhoods play a critical role in individual and community well-being. Where people live, especially where children grow up, is strongly correlated with important life outcomes, including physical and mental health, income, and intergenerational mobility.[8] Policymakers should treat housing as part of the overall social safety net, and fund it accordingly. Even in well-functioning markets, there will be some people who cannot afford decent quality, stable housing in safe, healthy neighborhoods without financial support. Policymakers and taxpayers should provide that support—both out of moral obligation and because the whole society benefits from a population that is well housed. The question is, then, what types of policies most effectively and efficiently help people attain stable housing in opportunity-rich places.

An action plan to achieve better housing systems—and a healthier society

Each chapter in this book identifies a key problem in current housing systems and offers a set of potential policy solutions. The chapters are designed to be read independently or out of order, if the reader chooses, but the whole is greater than the sum of the chapters. Many of the problems described are intertwined and cumulative. Trying to fix one problematic element of our housing system while ignoring the others can sometimes create greater economic harm—and raise more political opposition—than tackling several pieces at once. Most notably, because housing equity is the largest component of wealth for middle-class Americans, homeowners have strong financial incentives to resist any changes—like zoning reforms that allow lower-cost housing—that they perceive as threats to their property values.

The next chapter dives into limitations on new housing production. For the past thirty years, local governments across the United States have limited the market's ability to build enough homes in places where people most want to live. This pattern holds true both across metropolitan areas—housing construction greatly lags demand in the San Francisco Bay Area, New York City, and Greater Boston—and within metro areas. Affluent, high-opportunity neighborhoods within each metro are often the most resistant to building new homes, effectively using their local regulatory power to keep out newcomers. Collectively, limiting housing supply in the right places constrains economic opportunity, especially for people in the bottom half of the income distribution, and reinforces racial segregation. While the policy solutions here are relatively straightforward—reform excessively strict land use regulations—the politics of achieving better policies are wicked hard.

Chapter 3 looks at the flip side of this problem: the United States builds too many homes in locations that are environmentally vulnerable and/or damaging. Within large metro areas, most new housing is constructed at the urban fringe, far from job centers and public transportation, in car-dependent locations. Millions of homes have been built in parts of the country that frequently and predictably suffer from severe weather and natural disasters: areas adjacent to rivers and oceans that are prone to flooding, Western lands at high risk of wildfires. The harms wrought by climate change are not shared evenly: Black, Latino, and indigenous communities disproportionately occupy land that is at high risk of extreme heat, flooding, and other climate-related events. We are only beginning to witness the devastating financial and human costs of building homes in the "wrong" places—and yet we continue to do it. Solutions here need to come from all levels of government: clearer federal guidelines on which locations are at risk, more accurate risk pricing factored into home insurance and mortgages, revised state and local regulations prohibiting development in sensitive areas, and subsidies to relocate communities at high risk.

Chapter 4 focuses on the crucial role of housing in the larger context of social safety nets. Social insurance policies are meant to provide a minimum quality of life for all Americans, to catch people when unexpected bad events (health or family crises, recessions, natural disasters) make it temporarily impossible for them to support themselves. The United States has a stingier, less comprehensive social safety net than most rich countries. Housing is a gaping hole: unlike food stamps or Medicaid, poor families do not have a "right" to housing assistance—and most poor families receive no direct housing subsidies. Because this is primarily an income problem, not a housing problem, the most effective solution lies in giving poor people more money, whether by expanding existing tax credits or through creating new mechanisms, like a universal basic income. Tweaking the rules of existing housing subsidy programs to make them more effective and efficient is also worthwhile but in itself will not solve the problem.

Chapter 5 addresses the limitations of homeownership as a strategy for wealth-building. Currently, home equity is the largest single asset for most middle-income Americans. But this is risky for individual households because it concentrates rather than diversifies assets, while home equity can be difficult to access for short-term needs. Excess dependence on home equity fuels homeowners' opposition toward new development. Moreover, given America's long history of racial discrimination in housing and mortgage markets, homeownership is a major driver of persistent racial wealth gaps between Black and white Americans. The largest housing subsidy in the United States, the mortgage interest deduction, flows mostly to affluent white households, further exacerbating the racial wealth gap. Three types of changes would create a more balanced approach to asset-building: revise federal tax policy to target first-time home buyers; subsidize asset-building for low- and moderate-income households; and encourage all households to set aside short-term liquid savings.

Chapter 6 tackles the thorny problem of how to pay for all the goods and services that go along with new homes. Collectively, these items form the physical, economic, and social infrastructure of every community: roads and sidewalks, water and sewer systems, schools, child care facilities, libraries, and parks. Local governments shoulder primary responsibility for infrastructure construction, maintenance, and operation. Yet local governments have shallower pockets and less financial flexibility than state or federal governments. And because local communities vary enormously in their resources, a system that assigns local governments responsibility to finance infrastructure will create and reinforce vast inequalities across communities. It also creates fiscal and political incentives for local governments to resist construction of low-cost housing—feeding directly into restrictive land use policies discussed in chapter 2.

Chapter 7 explores how to move past the limits of localism. The United States is a federal political system; local decisionmaking has been baked into the country since its colonial past. Traditionally this is presented as a strength: local control enables a large and diverse population to create laws and policies that reflect communities' idiosyncratic preferences. In practice, local control over housing, schools, job centers, and infrastructure can lead to outcomes that are not socially optimal for regions, states, or the country. There is huge variation in local government capacity; many communities simply do not have the resources to plan and implement good policies. To address disparities, state and federal governments should set clear guidelines for local governments— from adequate housing production to climate protection—then provide financial support and technical assistance to localities that need it. Fiscal carrots and sticks may be necessary to change the behavior of localities that persist in discriminatory, anticompetitive practices.

Chapter 8 acknowledges the enormous political challenges involved in achieving better housing policies—and better housing outcomes for American families. Preferences over housing and land use don't align neatly with traditional partisan divides. Existing policies and programs have created winners who are invested in protecting the status quo. Homeowners who receive federal tax subsidies for their suburban, car-oriented lifestyles wield enormous influence over city councils and state legislatures, as do industry groups such as home builders and mortgage bankers. Even within the less visible world of affordable housing, non-profit organizations who benefit from existing subsidy programs tend to resist changes. The nascent prohousing movement has persuaded some cities and states to begin relaxing excessively strict land use regulations, although a coherent national movement has yet to take hold. Building political coalitions between younger, racially diverse renter households with affordable housing advocates could achieve broader, more durable policy improvements.

A few caveats

An important component of housing markets that this book does not address is the financial system that supports housing development and home purchases. This is such a large and complex topic that attempting to wrap it up in one chapter would be a gross oversimplification. Rather, readers who are interested in delving into the current housing finance system and possible reforms are encouraged to read the excellent work of other scholars on this topic.[9]

A book about housing is inherently a book about places. Several of the chapters lean more heavily toward large metropolitan areas, because those are the places where the breakdown in housing systems is most apparent, and where competition between neighboring local governments creates the most distortions. But excessively strict rules about housing development and affordability pressures are increasingly evident in smaller towns and some rural areas. Inadequate infrastructure financing, exposure to climate risk, and lack of support for low-income households are also universal problems. Where feasible, I discuss how the problems and policy solutions differ between central cities, suburbs, small towns, and rural areas.

Most problems discussed predate the COVID-19 pandemic, often by several decades, and will almost surely continue for many years to come. Nevertheless, COVID has raised some important questions about the future of housing and urban space. Will there be less demand to live in large, densely populated cities as a result of health concerns? What do optimal transportation systems look like, if work-from-home continues for an expanded share of the labor force? It is too early to know definitive answers to these questions, but these are important areas for future research.

2

Build More Homes Where People Want to Live

U.S. consumers rarely face shortages of essential goods and services. Supermarkets don't run out of bread or toilet paper (except before snowstorms or during global pandemics). If demand for a particular good or service increases—baking utensil sales spike as the *Great British Bake-Off* television show attains cult status, for instance—then companies that manufacture Bundt pans and pastry nozzles will make more of these items. Prices of hot items may increase in the short run, signaling firms to increase production, but we don't anticipate that consumers will have to queue for months or engage in bidding wars over limited supply. Simply put, households can find most of the things they need or want without worrying about scarcity.

If housing markets worked like the market for baking supplies, we would expect to see more new development in places where homes are currently expensive. High housing prices (or rents) indicate places where more people want to live, and where producers of housing (home builders and developers) could earn profits by building more homes. And yet, across U.S. cities and neighborhoods over the past thirty years, the places where housing was most expensive have generally built less new housing than moderately priced communities. Not enough additional homes have been built in locations with the highest demand, either across neighborhoods within a metro area or across metros.

In practice, housing markets work differently than those for most consumer goods. As previewed in chapter 1, they have some unusual features that make them prone to short-term imbalances between supply and demand. Some of these are inherent to the product—buildings are durable and fixed in place—while others reflect policy choices. A key policy choice is that in the U.S., housing production is regulated by local governments. Although development regulations vary widely in form and stringency across places, most cities and counties offer existing residents some opportunity to weigh in on proposals to build new housing—a feature not present in the production of most goods and services.

There are good reasons why governments regulate housing development, and why people who live in proximity to proposed growth should have an opportunity to weigh in. Adding more homes to a community affects the people who already live there—for better and for worse. In many places, increasing the number of homes will require replacing existing buildings with somewhat larger ones—a tangible change to the neighborhood's character. But there are also excellent reasons not to give current residents veto power, investing them with more authority than other stakeholders. How much housing gets built in what locations and at what cost impacts regional labor markets and our climate footprint. It also affects the degree to which low-income households have access to high-opportunity communities.

In many parts of the United States, the development process gives too much deference to current residents—especially affluent homeowners—who don't want their communities to change. But those preferences are imposing economic, environmental, and social costs on the rest of the country—especially on low-income people, Black and Latino families. Our housing production system must find a better balance between stagnation and progress, between placating incumbent owners and accommodating the needs of future generations.

Land is more expensive in places where people want to live

The price or rent for any given home reflects the cumulative value of the home's characteristics. Physical structure matters: the number of bedrooms and bathrooms, the architectural style, amenities like fireplaces and balconies. Much of the home's value comes from its location: proximity to subway stations and parks, or the quality of local public schools. Because the bundle of structural and location-specific characteristics is slightly different for each home, we can estimate the value of each separate element by comparing homes that differ along only one dimension. For instance, by comparing neighboring three-bedroom and four-bedroom homes, we can estimate how much people are willing to pay for one extra bedroom.

We can also decompose housing prices to understand the value that households place on location-specific amenities, for example, what people are willing to pay for land in different locations. That helps us predict where there is high demand for housing. Land near city centers or other large job clusters is more expensive than land at the urban fringe, because people will pay to avoid long commutes.[1] In densely populated cities with decent quality public transportation systems, land near subway stations or high-frequency bus lines is more expensive.[2] There isn't a price premium for land near transit in cities where public transportation is unreliable and driving is cheap and fast. Waterfront property sells for a premium in most places, from high-rise condos on Chicago's Lake Michigan shoreline to cottages along Santa Barbara's beaches.

People will also pay more to live in places where local government services improve their daily quality of life. Nearly all public school systems in the United States use geographic boundaries to determine "catchment" zones: where you live determines which school your child has the right to attend. (Many school systems allow children to attend out-of-zone schools if spaces are available; parents typically have to provide transportation and may have to pay extra fees.)[3] The perceived quality or desirability of different schools is capitalized into land values: the prices of structurally identical homes located on either side of catchment zone boundaries can vary enormously.[4] Other locally provided public services that affect land values include public safety (crime prevention), maintenance of roads and sidewalks, parks and recreational spaces, even something as mundane as reliable trash pickup.

Not every household has the same preferences over structure or location, of course. A single person who enjoys restaurants and museums is more likely to choose an apartment in a lively, center-city neighborhood, while a family with several young children will probably opt for a larger home in a high-quality school district. But there's enough consistency in which home features are desirable that we can estimate an average "price" associated with many characteristics—including to identify the locations in highest demand.

To make housing in desirable locations cheaper, use less land per home

If land is more expensive in desirable locations, does that imply that only millionaires can afford to live there? Does the natural operation of housing markets relegate middle- and low-income families to crime-ridden neighborhoods with lousy schools far away from jobs?

Not necessarily. Remember that the price (or rent) of an individual home is determined by the structural characteristics of the home (including size), the value of the land underneath it—and the amount of land the home uses. A person earning $50,000 can't outbid someone earning $200,000 for a house and yard of equal size. But if the less affluent person is willing to live in a smaller home that uses less land—especially an apartment in a multifamily building—they may be able to afford a home in the same neighborhood. Figure 2-1 shows how one lot could accommodate more housing: the same amount of land needed for one single-family detached house could accommodate several side-by-side townhouses or apartments in a low-rise multifamily building.

To understand how building more homes per lot can improve affordability, consider a simple example. The value of a typical residential lot in Wellesley, Massachusetts, an affluent suburb west of Boston, is $850,000.[5] Building a new single-family detached home would cost approximately $1.2 million, including construction materials, labor, engineering, finance, and other costs. So the total cost for a newly built single-family home would be roughly $2 million. Now imagine that a developer bought the same lot and, instead of one detached house, built five side-by-side townhouses. The per-unit development cost of these townhomes (including land) would be about $800,000—not cheap, but much less than $2 million. Most of the savings comes from the fact that land costs could be split among five home buyers, rather than borne entirely by one buyer. Building a four-story multifamily building with eleven condos would bring down the per unit costs to about $500,000—half the median value of existing homes in Wellesley.

Up to some threshold, adding more homes on expensive land reduces the cost of each individual home. Reducing the size of each home and stacking them vertically allows land costs to be shared across more households. In economic jargon, the developer is substituting capital for land: using more wood, steel, and concrete to build taller structures

FIGURE 2-1. More homes, less yard.

while reducing the amount of land per home. Building vertically increases the construction costs per square foot (think of adding elevators and switching from wood to steel), so developers will choose to do this only in places where land is expensive and households are willing to pay high rents or prices to live in that specific location.[6] Put another way, high-rise apartment buildings make financial sense in Manhattan and downtown San Francisco, where lots of people are willing to live in small homes close to jobs, restaurants, and museums. High-rise apartments don't make financial sense in most distant suburbs, small towns, or rural areas, where developers don't need to economize on land costs.

But homes come in many flavors besides the two extremes of single-family detached homes with yards and twenty-story apartment buildings. Most neighborhoods that were developed before the 1940s, when zoning became widespread, contain a mixture of building types and sizes. The Fan neighborhood in Richmond, Virginia, offers a good example: single-family detached homes are interspersed with rowhouses, four- and six-unit apartment buildings, nearly all less than four stories. These in-between housing types, sometimes called "gentle density," can provide smaller, lower-cost housing options than detached homes— where they are still legal to build.

A 30,000-foot view of the United States shows that city centers with expensive land tend to have higher density housing than distant suburbs or rural areas. But if we look more closely within metro areas, there are quite a few outliers: places with expensive land but relatively low housing density. For instance, the Kalorama neighborhood in Washington, DC, has some of the country's most expensive land—a quarter-acre lot is worth over $600,000, just for the land—but is mostly developed as single-family detached homes, and has built almost no new housing in the past thirty years.[7] Which raises the question—why?

Local governments exercise tight control over how much housing can be built where

In the United States, local governments have been delegated the authority to regulate housing supply. It is illegal to build a home on a piece of land—or to tear down or substantially alter a home that already exists—without getting permission from the city or county. A complex network of regulations governs what kinds of homes can be built in which locations, and what process property owners or developers have to follow in order to obtain permission. These regulations are hugely important in determining both the quantity and the price of housing available to consumers.

Local zoning laws form the core of housing regulations in nearly every city and county in the United States (Houston, the most famous exception, relies on private deed restrictions instead). Zoning regulates housing supply through four primary channels.[8] First, zoning laws divide the city or county into separate regions (called zones) that map onto designated geographic areas. Second, they specify what types of structures and land uses are permitted or prohibited in each zone. For instance, an R1 residential zone would typically allow only single-family detached homes, while commercial zones would allow offices and stores, and an agricultural zone would only allow structures necessary for farming-related activities. Third, zoning laws set out dimensional requirements for all structures, such as maximum building height or minimum lot size and width.

Fourth, and perhaps most importantly, zoning laws set out the process for obtaining permission to build new structures. A key distinction is whether development is allowed "by right" or requires discretionary approvals.[9] By-right development means that proposals for development can be reviewed and approved by administrative staff, as long as the proposals conform with use type and dimensional requirements. On the other hand, some types of development are required to go through a more extensive review process, sometimes called "conditional use" or "special use." The process for obtaining conditional use approvals varies widely across localities but often requires the developer to present the proposal at public meetings.[10] These meetings offer residents an opportunity to voice concerns or objections to the proposal.

On the face of it, local governments exercising control over the type and size of structures that can be built in various parts of the community seems innocuous enough. Cities and towns have always tried to limit the location of noisy, smelly, or otherwise unpleasant activities; in the early nineteenth century, cities required that slaughterhouses, tanneries, and breweries be located downwind and downstream from where residents lived.[11] Tall, bulky buildings limit sunlight that reaches people on the streets and in shorter neighboring buildings. Building codes emerged from tangible concerns over health and safety, like the need for fire escapes. The push for more community engagement in the development process emerged from progressive activists in the 1960s and 1970s, in reaction to federal urban renewal projects that displaced low-income, Black and Latino communities without giving them the opportunity to speak.[12]

However, research shows that people who participate in community meetings are hardly representative of "the community": older, affluent white homeowners tend to dominate the proceedings, even when they constitute a minority of residents.[13] These homeowners generally perceive new development—especially of moderately priced housing—as a threat to their property values. Chapters 5 and 6 discuss why this is such a strong motivation to oppose new development, and some ways to mitigate the incentives. Reliably antidevelopment constituents who fight vociferously against any changes to "neighborhood character" have earned the nickname "Not In My Backyard," or NIMBY. Chapter 8 discusses an emerging countermovement that advocates for relaxing constraints on new housing and has dubbed itself YIMBY (Yes In My Backyard).

There are clear social and economic costs to the way many local governments currently regulate housing supply—costs that are largely borne by lower-income, younger, and nonwhite households. The clearest example is disparities in how zoning laws treat different types of residential structures. Nearly every U.S. city and county zones a majority of land exclusively for single-family detached homes, with much smaller areas zoned for all other housing types.[14] As discussed in the previous section, using more land per home increases the price of the home, especially where land is expensive. Zoning that prohibits everything except single-family detached homes—from rowhouses and duplexes all the way to high-rise apartment buildings—prevents developers from creating lower-cost housing options in high-demand locations. Towns like Wellesley, Massachusetts, effectively use zoning to turn themselves into gated communities: only people who can afford to buy million-dollar single-family homes on large lots can move into the community. Developers could profitably build smaller, less expensive homes in Wellesley, and many more households would like to move there—but Wellesley's current residents have created policies that make this impossible.

While single-family-exclusive zoning is the most obvious (and most prevalent) way in which land use regulations inhibit housing supply, nearly all the components of zoning can be weaponized to block lower-cost housing. Affluent suburbs across New England require minimum lot sizes as high as two acres per home, forcing developers to use more land than they would otherwise choose—particularly onerous where land is expensive.[15] Most of California's suburbs cap building heights at three stories, so that even where apartment buildings are technically allowed, they are financially infeasible.[16] While single-family homes are generally allowed by right in residential areas, zoning more often treats multifamily buildings as a conditional use, requiring developers to work through a series of complex and expensive processes to receive approval—while creating plenty of opportunities for existing residents to protest.[17]

Collectively, all these restrictions on housing supply—especially on apartment buildings and other small, dense housing types—reduce the number of homes that are built and increase housing costs, relative to what markets would have provided otherwise. That is, zoning distorts

market outcomes in ways that make housing scarcer and more expensive. Not every community faces the same degree of distortion: whether
zoning is a binding constraint on housing supply, and to what extent,
depends on the interaction between local zoning laws and underlying
market factors. A zoning law in rural Texas that prohibits high-rise
apartment buildings has little true impact on housing markets, because
the economics make vertical construction unattractive even without
zoning. But limits on housing density in high-demand neighborhoods—
places like Greenwich Village in Manhattan, Kalorama in Washington,
DC, and San Marino, California—create enormous distortions.

Measuring "excessively strict" zoning is like holding a moonbeam in your hand

State and federal policymakers are increasingly interested in using
fiscal carrots and sticks to encourage local governments to relax unnec-
essarily strict zoning.[18] To implement that approach, policymakers need
to be able to measure zoning stringency, to compare strictness across
geographic areas and changes over time. But that's a tricky task. There
are thousands of zoning laws adopted by cities, townships, and counties
across the United States. Most zoning laws are hundreds of pages long,
written in complex legal language. Deciding which provisions embedded
in those complex legal documents are "too strict" requires considerable
judgment and expertise. If state and federal governments want to make
funding contingent on localities adopting "better" zoning, it will be essential to develop accurate, fair, transparent metrics.

Broadly speaking, researchers have relied on three approaches to
measuring zoning stringency: surveys of local planners, reviewing
and coding legal documents, or inferring stringency from observable
housing market data. Each of these methods has distinct strengths and
weaknesses.[19] Surveys can pick up useful insights into local officials'
perceptions about the difficulty of building homes in their jurisdictions,
but they are expensive to administer, often have low response rates, and

are inherently subjective. Reading and manually coding zoning laws is extremely labor intensive and cannot capture the ways in which zoning rules on paper differ from how rules are applied in practice.

The third approach, inferring zoning restrictiveness from housing market outcomes, relies on economic theory. Comparing real-world data on housing prices and production levels against predictions of how well-functioning housing markets should work allows us to identify places that are out of equilibrium. Are there places where the housing demand is strong, based on economic fundamentals, but housing supply isn't keeping up? Where are housing prices high and rising over time, but little additional housing has been built? These questions are relatively straightforward to answer with data and can serve as an initial guide to places where zoning is constraining housing development.

Decades of painstaking research on zoning by economists and urban planners have produced a high degree of consensus on which places in the United States have tight land use regulations, regardless of the methods used to measure zoning. One of the most reliable indicators of restrictive zoning turns out to be a very intuitive measure: places where housing prices (or rents) are high relative to household income almost always have restrictive zoning.

Exclusionary zoning exists everywhere, but it creates the most damage in large coastal metros

If excessively restrictive zoning were limited to a handful of places, then the housing market impacts would largely be felt in the immediate community or a few adjacent communities. And indeed the extent of tight zoning—how much it restricts housing supply—varies widely across the country. To think about how big a problem zoning is, and where its impacts cause the most damage, we can break down the United States into three levels of geography: across metropolitan areas, across cities and counties within metro areas, and across neighborhoods within cities or counties.

Starting at the highest geographic level, overly restrictive zoning is most prevalent and most problematic along the West Coast and the Northeast corridor from Washington, DC, to Boston.[20] Looking at the ratio of median housing prices to median household income shows these geographic patterns: housing is most expensive relative to income in the Boston, New York, and Portland metro areas, as well as coastal California (figure 2-2). These areas include some of the strongest regional labor markets in the United States, with well-paid jobs in growing industries that attract highly educated workers.

Not all metros with strong labor markets suffer from high housing costs relative to incomes. Sunbelt metros from Atlanta to Houston to

FIGURE 2-2. Housing affordability varies widely across U.S. metro areas.
Median home value-to-income ratios, 100 largest metro areas, 2018.

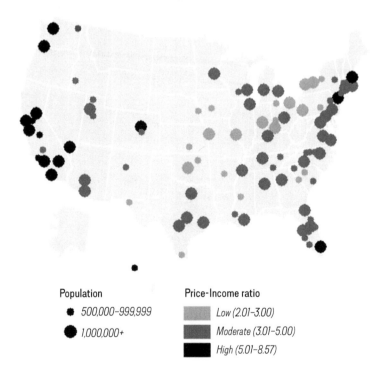

Population
- 500,000–999,999
- 1,000,000+

Price-Income ratio
- Low (2.01–3.00)
- Moderate (3.01–5.00)
- High (5.01–8.57)

Source: U.S. Census Bureau 2018 American Community Survey, one-year estimates, tables B25077 and B19013.

Phoenix have also seen strong job growth but have built enough additional housing to accommodate this growth, while housing prices remained relatively stable. Most local governments in these metro areas have taken a more relaxed approach to regulating housing development—with some exceptions, discussed later in the chapter. (Housing growth patterns in Sunbelt metros do raise environmental concerns, as discussed in chapter 3, and the lack of reliable public transportation means that most households are required to incur the expense of owning cars, partially offsetting lower housing costs.)

One caveat about using housing price to income ratios to infer zoning restrictiveness is that we cannot distinguish whether low housing demand places have "tight" zoning rules on paper. Metro areas like St. Louis, Buffalo, and Flint, Michigan, have seen slow population growth for decades and so haven't needed to build much additional housing (some newly built housing may be needed to replace older homes in poor condition). Zoning rules like bans on apartment buildings or requirements for large minimum lot sizes don't actively constrain housing supply if demand for new homes is low. This dynamic is similar for many rural parts of the United States, which have been losing population since the mid-twentieth century. Both slow-growth metros and rural areas suffer from poor housing quality (a function of older homes in need of maintenance), inadequate infrastructure, and high vacancy rates. These are serious problems, but not directly related to zoning, so they require a different suite of policy solutions.

When viewed from the 30,000-foot level, restrictive zoning and the resulting high housing costs appear to be primarily regional or state problems.[21] But if we zoom in to look at individual metro areas, we can see that even moderately priced metros have some unusually expensive localities—places where zoning is used as a tool to limit access by lower-income households. Figure 2-3 shows four metro areas with substantially different housing market dynamics: Dallas, Detroit, Los Angeles, and Washington, DC. While the Dallas and Detroit metro areas overall have moderate housing prices, both metros have some exclusive

FIGURE 2-3. Rents vary widely within metro areas.

Distribution of median rents by local jurisdiction.

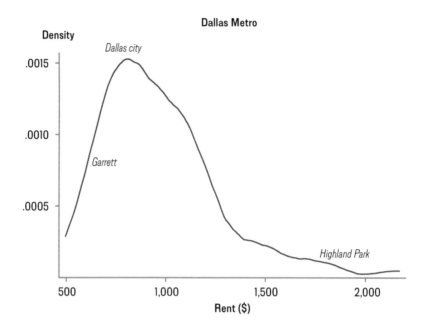

Dallas Metro

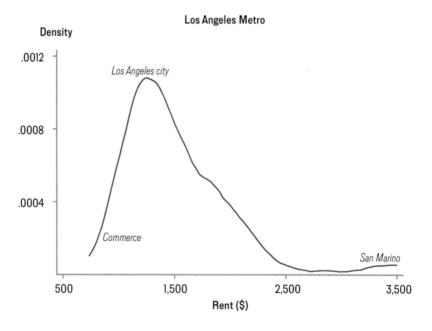

Los Angeles Metro

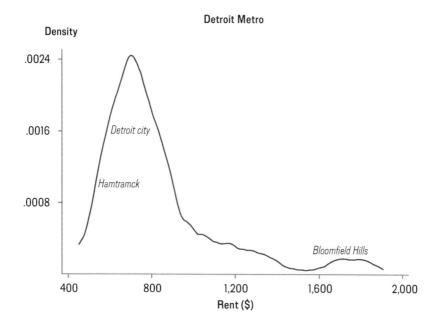

Detroit Metro

Density

.0024

.0016   Detroit city

Hamtramck

.0008

Bloomfield Hills

400   800   1,200   1,600   2,000

Rent ($)

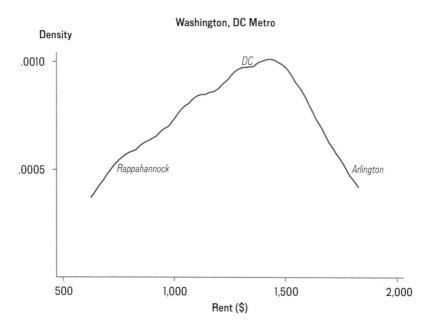

Washington, DC Metro

Density

.0010   DC

.0005   Rappahannock   Arlington

500   1,000   1,500   2,000

Rent ($)

Source: U.S. Census Bureau 2017 American Community Survey, five-year estimates, table B25064.

Note: Each graph shows the kernel density of median rents for incorporated
places within the metro area.

suburban communities (Highland Park in Dallas, Bloomfield Hills in Detroit), where housing costs are out of reach for the typical household in the metro area.

The same pattern is also visible across neighborhoods within individual cities or counties (at least among large jurisdictions). Some parts of zoning laws are consistent across all parts of the political jurisdiction—procedural rules tend to be similar for the same types of projects—but there is tremendous variation across neighborhoods in how much land is zoned for apartments and the dimensional requirements, such as lot size and building height. Affluent, predominantly white neighborhoods within cities tend to restrict development to single-family detached homes. Outside the downtown core, they also limit commercial activity (such as grocery stores and coffee shops) on residential streets—quite similar to their suburban neighbors. Because many affluent urban neighborhoods were fully developed as low-density housing in the mid-twentieth century, leaving no open space, they have little if any capacity to add housing under current zoning.

Washington, DC, offers a useful example of the within-city dynamics. The District has experienced a housing boom over the past decade—averaging nearly 4,300 new housing units per year—but development has been highly concentrated in a handful of neighborhoods. Previously moderate-income, mostly Black neighborhoods like Columbia Heights, Shaw, and U Street have been transformed by large apartment and condo buildings. Meanwhile, some of the most affluent and expensive parts of the District—places like Kalorama, Georgetown, and Cleveland Park—have built almost no new housing.[22] These neighborhoods were largely developed as single-family homes in the early to mid-twentieth century (or before, in parts of Georgetown), and have little extra zoned capacity today. Locking in low-density housing through zoning laws, combined with tools like historic preservation, make it difficult if not impossible to increase the number of homes in these neighborhoods, even as the District grows around them. Low-density zoning creates implicit price insurance for property owners: only people wealthy enough to afford large homes can move into these neighborhoods.

Restrictive zoning most directly impacts the availability and price of newly built housing, which is a relatively small part of the overall housing stock. Limiting supply has spillover effects on the prices and rents of existing homes too. Newly built homes are more expensive than older homes, conditional on size and location. Like other forms of durable capital, homes depreciate over time, as appliances, materials, and building systems experience wear and tear from everyday use. In housing markets with ample new construction, the highest-income households move into newly built homes that are the top of the housing food chain, while older homes "filter down" in price over time and are occupied by middle- and lower-income households.[23] When zoning limits the amount of new construction, higher-income households occupy the best available older homes, interrupting the process of downward filtering, and pushing middle- and lower-income households into poorer quality buildings. In the most tightly regulated markets, older homes can "filter up" and become more expensive—a process exemplified by blocks of meticulously renovated brownstones in Harlem and Brooklyn.

Not building homes in the right places has economic, environmental, and human costs

Restrictive zoning doesn't just have harmful impacts on housing markets. The cost and availability of housing interact with labor markets, transportation systems, and economic opportunity more broadly. In regions where housing is expensive, employers have to offer higher salaries to attract and retain good workers. Not building enough homes at diverse price points in close proximity to major job centers is particularly damaging, as the Los Angeles region illustrates. The west side of Los Angeles along Wilshire Boulevard forms one of the region's densest job corridors, with large employers like UCLA, several medical centers,

and the corporate office of Fox Studios. The adjacent residential areas of
Brentwood, Westwood, and Beverly Hills feature very restrictive zoning
and some of the region's most expensive housing. Food service workers,
housekeepers, and lower-wage medical staff cannot afford to live close
to their workplaces and must commute long distances from cheaper
neighborhoods, many of which are not well served by public transportation. The additional time and money spent commuting, as well as
harmful greenhouse gas (GHG) emissions, are indirect costs imposed by
wealthy Westside communities' tight housing regulations.

This scenario also illustrates how restrictive zoning in wealthy areas
reinforces economic and racial segregation. Because low-wage workers
can't afford to rent homes in West L.A., they can't send their children
to the high-quality public schools in those exclusive wealthy neighborhoods. Research shows that where people live is strongly correlated with
intergenerational mobility: children who grow up in places with lower
residential segregation and less income inequality tend to do better as
adults than their parents.[24] Children who move to low-poverty neighborhoods when they are young have higher incomes as adults—an outcome
that benefits the entire country.[25] Adults also benefit from the opportunity to move to low-poverty neighborhoods, experiencing better mental
health outcomes from living in a safer and less stressful environment.[26]

Across the United States, Black and Latino households have substantially lower incomes and wealth than non-Hispanic white households
and are much more likely to rent their homes. (The income gap between
Asian and white households is less consistent, varying by geography.)
Zoning restrictions on multifamily housing in neighborhoods like Westwood and Beverly Hills may not be intended to restrict access to Black
and Latino families, but they certainly have that effect.

Solutions

Finding policy solutions to exclusionary zoning can be divided into two separate sets of questions. First, what do better land use policies and better housing outcomes look like? Second, what kind of fiscal, legal, or political levers could be used to nudge local governments to adopt better policies? Here I address the first question (the "what"). Chapters 6, 7, and 8 tackle the thornier question of the institutional impediments to adopting better policies.

Two clear principles for better land use policies, many variations in implementation

Because local housing markets vary so widely—in land values, existing housing structures and density, and current land use regulations—it is impossible to develop one simple template or prescription for "good" zoning. Rather, zoning reforms should embrace two key principles. First, each jurisdiction should allow a diverse range of residential structure types and home sizes. Second, the development process should be simpler, shorter, and more transparent.

Exactly what "better" zoning would look like will vary across places. Looking at two communities in the Boston suburbs illustrates why. Wellesley is a residential suburb that currently reserves most of its land exclusively for single-family detached homes on one-acre lots. It could diversify its stock—and reduce average housing prices—by reducing the minimum lot size for single-family detached homes to a quarter acre and adding rowhouses and duplexes to the structure types permitted "as of right" (does not require discretionary approval). The inner suburb of Somerville was largely developed before World War II, and much of its residential land has three-unit apartment buildings with one unit per floor (known as triple-deckers), single-family homes on small lots of less than two thousand square feet, and low-rise apartment buildings. So "relaxing" zoning in Somerville would require changes such as increasing building height limits (most are capped at three stories), easing other dimensional requirements (such as floor-to-area ratios), and allowing development as of right, rather than by special permit.

Prescribing zoning reforms for large cities is even more complex: big cities generally allow a wide range of structure types and home sizes in commercial districts and some residential areas, while tightly restricting density in the most affluent parts of the city. In New York City and Washington, DC, zoning rules allow redeveloping rowhouses and low-rise apartment buildings into higher-density apartments in moderate-income neighborhoods, but they prohibit almost any higher-density redevelopment in high-income neighborhoods. That approach creates more risk of displacement among economically vulnerable renters, while insulating wealthy homeowners from any unwanted changes. Meaningful improvements to affordability will require cities either to adopt consistent citywide revisions (e.g., legalize apartments across all residential areas) or to focus the push for increased density in high-opportunity neighborhoods. This choice between strategies may rely more on political considerations than policy design.

Localities should target better housing outcomes, not just better policies on paper

Focusing on what policies local governments change on paper misses the larger goal: zoning reform is not an end unto itself but the means to better housing outcomes. Defining better outcomes and setting concrete benchmarks would help local governments, housing advocates, and potentially state and federal agencies to measure progress. Mayors and county supervisors often run for office promising vague or unrealistic improvements ("ending homelessness" or "making housing more affordable"), but campaign statements are rarely helpful in measuring day-to-day improvements.

In-demand communities should aim to increase both the total amount of housing and the diversity of homes, while lowering housing costs. A diverse housing stock is essential to supporting an economically and demographically diverse population. A wealthy suburb that allows only five-bedroom, single-family detached homes on one-acre lots could expand its population size by building more of the same, but it would remain accessible only to wealthy families. Allowing a diverse range of structure types, lot sizes, and home sizes, both for rental and for sale, would expand the range of housing choices—and reduce the price of entry into that community. Zoning isn't the only reason that households of similar income tend to cluster together; some degree of geographic sorting by income reflects similar preferences over amenities, including public services. But zoning rules that lock in low-density housing prevent neighborhoods from evolving to accommodate economic and demographic changes. Predominantly owner-occupied communities should reduce barriers to rental housing, such as zoning bans on apartment buildings as well as occupancy restrictions that prohibit roommates from sharing homes.

Beyond equity concerns, making zoning more flexible and responsive to changes in housing demand helps regional labor markets work. In theory, a metro area in which each city and county "specialized" in one type of housing—expensive mansions in one town, moderately priced townhouses in another, subsidized apartments in a third—could collectively provide enough housing at different price points to serve all the region's workers, from CEOs to housekeepers. In practice, neither jobs nor moderately priced housing is distributed evenly throughout metro areas. For instance, many of the job-rich areas in Chicago are located on the north side of the city, whereas lower-cost housing is concentrated on the south and west sides. Local governments face financial pressures to resist building lower-priced housing, as discussed in chapters 6 and 7. But allowing housing at a range of price points within every community helps the larger regional economy.

Because developing housing is a long process, and new construction is a small share of total housing stock, benchmarks for improvement should measure both short-term, intermediate steps as well as longer-

term achievements. An increase in the number of building permit applications and approvals will be visible long before newly built homes are
completed. To measure improvement in the development process (transparency and efficiency), localities should track the share of projects that
are approved as of right, without requiring waivers of existing rules,
and the length of time projects take to complete stages in the development process (permit application to permit approval to construction
completion).

As long as land use regulation is entirely a matter of local control, it
will be impossible to achieve widespread zoning reform. Every community has a bloc of existing homeowners who passionately resist changes
to their neighborhood—and who are willing to devote time, energy,
money, and political capital to fighting proposed reforms. Mayors, city
councilors, and county supervisors are reluctant to oppose the "no
change" bloc, even if they understand the need for and (privately) support zoning reform. Most individual cities and towns are relatively small
players within their metro area's housing market. Even if a few communities manage to enact prohousing reforms in their localities, it won't be
enough to budge regional housing production or affordability.

To make meaningful progress on increasing the supply of moderately
priced housing, there must be some accountability to higher levels of
government (either state or federal). Chapters 6 and 7 discuss the kinds
of tools that could support well-intentioned local governments in developing and implementing better housing policies—and how to hold
persistently exclusionary places accountable.

Conclusion

Reforming zoning won't solve all housing affordability problems
overnight. Two caveats are important to avoid overselling the benefits
of better land use policy. First, housing availability and affordability in
high-demand places will take time to show substantial improvement,

even if large-scale zoning reform were to happen tomorrow. Many parts of the United States have underbuilt housing for decades. New construction takes time, even under a more streamlined process. But continuing to stick with our broken system is guaranteed to make matters worse.

Second, there will always be some households that earn too little income to afford market-rate housing without direct subsidies. The public sector needs to provide increased financial support for poor households, in ways that better allow them access to high-opportunity communities. Zoning reform is necessary, but it is just half of the equation needed to improve housing stability for low-income Americans.

3

Stop Building Homes in the Wrong Places

Every year, the social, economic, and human costs of climate change become more tangible.[1] Wildfire season in the western United States grows longer and deadlier. Hurricanes along the Atlantic and Gulf coasts have become more intense. Extreme heat and rainfall damage property and threaten economic activity across the country. While no part of the United States has gone untouched by climate damage, the costs are disproportionately borne by low-income, Black, Latino, and Native communities.

The United States continues to build—and rebuild—too many homes in the wrong places, environmentally speaking. Since the 1950s, most new housing in the United States has been built in low-density suburbs, far from downtown job clusters and public transportation. Single-family homes—the predominant structure type in suburban areas—have a larger carbon footprint than apartment buildings. The United States allows and even subsidizes housing development in locations that face a high risk of recurring damage from wildfires, hurricanes, floods, water stress, and other climate-related challenges.

National conversations around climate change tend to focus on high-level solutions: creating a carbon tax; shifting energy sources away from fossil fuels (coal, natural gas) and toward renewable sources (solar, wind); adhering to international climate treaties (Kyoto, Paris); creating clean energy jobs. All these approaches are necessary for large-scale change, yet public debate rarely addresses how they might affect communities on the ground. Implementing many of these policy changes successfully will require changes in people's daily lives—a topic that receives far less attention from media and policymakers.

To illustrate why housing and land use policies matter, consider how people might change their behavior in response to a carbon tax, which is intended to discourage polluting behaviors like driving. Three-quarters of Americans commute from home to work by driving alone, while only 5 percent use public transit, because public transportation across most of the United States offers infrequent and unreliable service.[2] In economists' theoretical models, a carbon tax should nudge people to move closer to their workplaces, or to locations with better subway and bus service. Developers would respond to increased demand for those locations by building more homes. In reality, as we saw in chapter 2, local governments have adopted policies that make it difficult to build housing in many job-rich, transit-accessible locations. Building new subway or light rail lines to areas not currently served by transit requires navigating the same complicated process as building more housing. In short, creating a carbon tax that makes driving more expensive without addressing policy constraints on housing development could impose financial burdens on lower-income workers while being less effective at reducing vehicle emissions.

Americans' environmentally unfriendly choices of where to live and how to move around are not entirely the result of market forces. Federal policy subsidizes our behavior through a variety of channels, including mortgage underwriting, transportation funding, and disaster recovery programs. Individuals' out-of-pocket costs for their housing and transportation choices do not fully reflect the environmental damage that they cause, or the risks that they incur. In economic terms, our urban development patterns are riddled with incorrectly priced externalities.

To nudge Americans toward better behavior will require overhauling federal, state, and local policies in some politically challenging ways.

Large homes in car-dependent suburbs create large environmental footprints

Where people live—in which region of the country, which city, even which neighborhood—directly affects how they impact the environment. One way to measure this is through household carbon footprints, which are derived from people's consumption of energy. Transportation and household energy are the two largest components of household carbon footprints.[3] The typical suburban household has a substantially larger carbon footprint than households in the urban core of the same metro area, because suburban households drive more and live in larger homes.

The transportation part of our footprint depends on how far we travel and what mode of transportation we choose. A two-mile round trip to the grocery store driving an SUV emits more greenhouse gasses (GHGs) than driving the same distance in a Prius, which in turn emits more GHGs than cycling or walking. A bus or subway traveling two miles uses a lot of energy, but it generally transports many passengers, so the per-person footprint of public transit is lower than driving in a single-occupancy vehicle.

To think about how far people travel in a typical day, we can break out the types of trips they make and the distance between starting and ending points. The median commute is now over ten miles one way.[4] Much of the focus on travel patterns concentrates on travel between home and work, but a substantial amount of travel is for noncommuting purposes. Dropping off and picking up children from school; swinging by the supermarket, dry cleaner, and hardware store; or heading out for dinner and a movie with friends collectively make up more than 80 percent of daily trips.[5] Noncommuting trips are a larger share of overall travel for women than for men.

Both mode choice and distances traveled are closely correlated with where people live. These relationships are obvious with commuting. Residents of Chicago neighborhoods like Lakeview and Kenwood, within five to ten miles of the Loop, can commute to downtown on the Chicago Transit Authority's L (elevated) rail or bus system. Coworkers who live in outer-ring suburbs like Schaumburg or Oswego have both longer distances to travel and few alternatives to driving. Public transit systems in the United States are scarcer and offer less frequent service than in other developed countries. Even in the New York metro area, which has the most extensive transit network, nearly half of commuters drive alone to work, compared to about one-third who used transit (figure 3-1). Transit ridership is lower in metro areas where a large share of jobs are located outside traditional downtowns, because most transit systems are designed around suburb-to-downtown commutes, rather than "reverse commuting" or suburb-to-suburb trips.

Location matters for nonwork travel too. Neighborhoods where the street grid was largely built before cars and trucks became widespread tend to have a more compact form—a pattern that holds even in sprawling metro areas. The Inman Park neighborhood of Atlanta was originally built in the 1890s on the streetcar line to downtown, one of many "streetcar suburbs" built during this era.[6] Street segments between intersections are relatively short, lined with sidewalks on both sides, making it easier, safer, and more convenient for people to walk. Stores and services are closer to residential areas, allowing people to run daily errands and socialize without needing to drive.

Land use patterns in Sandy Spring, an Atlanta suburb built in the 2000s, are much more car oriented. Most Sandy Spring homes are located in exclusively residential neighborhoods, with stores and services located in commercial areas several miles away. Winding cul-de-sacs typical of suburban subdivisions mean a longer effective distance between two points than the pre-car street grid—therefore a longer travel time for pedestrians or cyclists.[7] The absence of sidewalks, crosswalks, and protected bike lanes increases the risk of injury from car crashes.[8]

FIGURE 3-1. Driving alone dominates commuting in large, urbanized areas.
Travel mode share for fifteen largest urbanized areas, 2018.

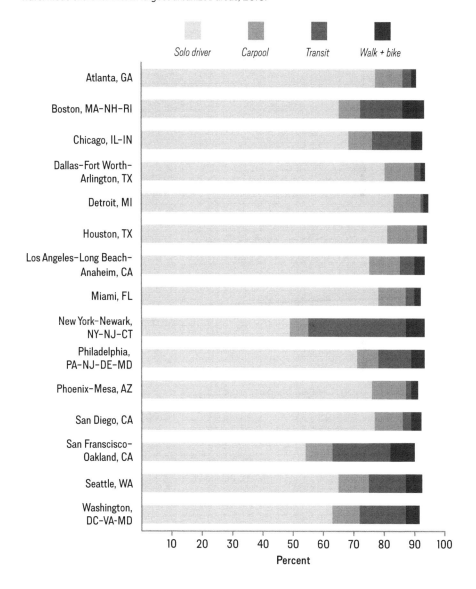

Source: U.S. Census Bureau 2018 American Community Survey, one-year estimates, table S0802.

Note: Excludes "Other" travel mode and respondents who work from home.

Shrinking our climate footprints doesn't require all (or even most) households to give up driving. But we should aim to increase the feasibility of car-light lifestyles, in which households can achieve more of their daily activities without a car, or by driving shorter distances. Building more homes in mixed-use neighborhoods that are close to job centers, with access to reliable public transit, and street design that is conducive to walking and cycling would allow people to shift from car-dependent to car-light lifestyles, thus reducing their carbon footprint. Owning and maintaining a car is expensive, so enabling people to drive less, and reducing the number of cars owned per household, can translate into substantial savings.

Besides transportation, people's climate footprint reflects the amount of energy they consume in their homes. Major items include heating and air conditioning, water heaters, and appliances such as dishwashers, refrigerators, and clothes dryers. Larger homes require more energy for heating and cooling. The kitchen of a 3,000-square-foot house can hold many more electronic gadgets than the kitchen in a one-bedroom apartment. Multi-unit buildings have smaller homes than single-family detached structures, leading to lower energy usage per household. Conditional on home size, newly built houses tend to be more energy efficient—think of drafty, single-paned, wood-framed windows versus new double-paned ones with vinyl or fiberglass frames. Household carbon footprints vary widely across regions within the United States, reflecting differences in the average daily need for heat and air-conditioning, as well as relative dirtiness of energy sources (coal-fired power plants and natural gas versus nuclear, solar, or wind).

The most environmentally friendly way for cities and towns to grow in population is to create modest-sized, compactly built, energy-efficient housing within walking distance of shops and services, and if possible, near existing bus or rail stations. And yet, most new housing in the United States is exactly the opposite: single-family detached homes, built in suburban or exurban neighborhoods that enforce strict separation between homes and commercial areas and have minimal access to public transit. As figure 3-2 shows, each decade since 1950 has seen higher growth rates in suburban and exurban counties than centrally located counties. This pattern is consistent across all regions of the country and for nearly every large metro area—including metros where overall population growth has been flat.

FIGURE 3-2. Suburban and exurban counties are growing faster than the urban core.
Percentage change in housing units for metropolitan counties, 1940–2010.

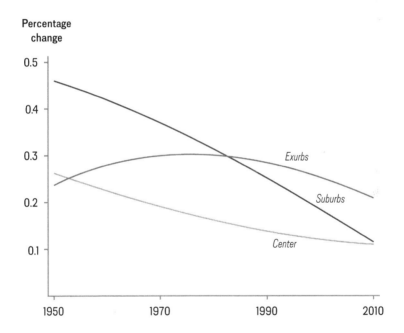

Source: Author calculations using Steven Manson, Jonathan Schroeder, David Van Riper, Tracy Kugler, and Steven Ruggles. IPUMS National Historical Geographic Information System: Version 16.0 (dataset), http://doi.org/10.18128/D050.V16.0.

Note: Graph shows percentage change in housing from prior decade (e.g., 1950 shows change from 1940 to 1950).

Housing policies should reflect that exposure to climate change varies across places

The second type of "wrong" place to build homes is in locations with elevated risks of recurring damage from climate change. All parts of the United States have already experienced harm from climate change. Loss of life and property damage from intense storms and wildfires are the clearest examples. The financial and human costs of climate change are projected to grow over time, even if governments adopt more aggressive adaptation and mitigation strategies.[9] Understanding how the type and likelihood of climate hazards vary across places would help households, the real estate industry, and policymakers reduce harm to people, communities, and the economy.

To think about the interactions between housing supply and climate change, we can break out different categories of climate hazards and consider geographic variation in exposure to these categories, shown in table 3-1. Public attention often focuses on high-visibility, acute hazards, like hurricanes and wildfires. The probability of experiencing severe storms varies widely across places. The annual probability of a hurricane is six times greater in Florida and three times greater in Texas than in the combined states of Pennsylvania, New Jersey, Maryland, Delaware, and Virginia.[10]

Other hazards manifest more like chronic diseases: harms rise incrementally and therefore may not be immediately apparent.[11] Rising sea levels have caused frequent inundation (flooding) in places like Norfolk, Virginia, and much of South Florida—not just during storms, but periodically throughout the year.[12] Extreme heat—prolonged periods of very hot temperatures—poses serious health threats, especially to older adults and people with underlying health issues. A heat wave in June 2021 caused several hundred excess deaths—mortalities above what would typically occur—across Oregon and Washington, states with usually mild summers where many homes lack air conditioning.[13] In 2017, air traffic in Phoenix was suspended for three days due to extreme

TABLE 3-1. Severe weather risks vary across U.S. regions.
Regional variation in types of weather events, 1992–2013.

WEATHER EVENT	REGION
Drought	Midwest, Southwest
Fire	West
Flood	Pacific Northwest, Midwest, South
Hurricane	Atlantic Coast, Gulf Coast
Severe storm	Northeast, South, Midwest, Central Plains
Winter storm	Northeast, South, Midwest, Pacific Northwest

Source: P. Romero-Lankao and others, "2014: North America." In *Climate Change 2014: Impacts, Adaptation, and Vulnerability,* "Part B: Regional Aspects. Contribution of Working Group II to the Fifth Assessment Report of the Intergovernmental Panel on Climate Change," V. R. Barros and others (eds.), Intergovernmental Panel on Climate Change, pp. 1439–1498, www.ipcc.ch/site/assets/uploads/2018/02/WGIIAR5-Chap26_FINAL.pdf.

heat.[14] Flooding due to extreme rainfall is a likely harm for large swathes of the eastern U.S. and the Pacific Northwest. Several of the largest urban areas, including the New York metro, Chicagoland, and Southern California also face elevated risk for water stress.[15]

Climate change impacts housing markets through several channels, both directly and indirectly. Homes sustain physical damage from water, wind, fire, and extreme temperatures (both heat and cold). As climate risks becomes more visible, people will be less willing to buy homes located in high-risk locations, making it difficult for current owners to sell, and causing property values to fall.[16] Climate risk has not yet systematically affected the ability of property owners to buy insurance or take out mortgages, due in part to federal government policies, but that is likely to change over time. In many metro areas, low-income, Black and brown households form a disproportionate share of long-term property owners in high-risk locations; therefore climate-related property value declines will exacerbate racial wealth gaps.[17]

Climate change imposes large costs on local and state governments,

who share responsibility for maintaining a wide range of physical infrastructure (as discussed in chapter 6). Superstorm Sandy provides a clear
example of the types of costs borne by local and state agencies after
acute climate events: repairing and upgrading roads, bridges, subway
and commuter rail systems, water infrastructure, parks, and public
buildings. Longer-term pressures such as water stress and extreme heat
will also require investments and adjustments by cities and counties.
Local and state governments differ widely in their capacity to prepare
for and recover from climate harms, a point illustrated by comparing
recovery efforts following Hurricane Katrina and Superstorm Sandy.[18]

Despite overwhelming evidence that climate hazards are worsen-
ing, the United States continues to allow—and subsidize—new housing
development in high-risk areas. South Florida, Houston, and Phoenix
are among the fastest growing urban areas, yet all face a high risk of
multiple climate threats. In 2018, 42 percent of the U.S. population lived
in coastal shoreline counties—areas especially vulnerable to coastal
storms and sea level rise—although these counties constitute only 10
percent of U.S. land area.[19] Over the past several decades, the appeal of
living near oceans has driven increased population growth in coastal
areas, prompting development of more, and more expensive, homes.[20]
Yet policies like the National Flood Insurance Program (NFIP) and federal mortgage guarantees don't accurately reflect the climate risks associated with these locations.

Burdens of climate change fall heavily on low-income, Black and brown communities

Just as the distribution of climate risk varies across geographic areas,
both the likelihood and the severity of harm from climate change are
not felt equally among all population groups. Persistent disparities in
financial resources, social networks, and political power—the result of
decades of discrimination—place low-income, Black, Latino, and Native
communities at higher risk.[21]

Low-income people live where land and housing are relatively cheap—which often means higher-risk locations.[22] In cities like New Orleans and Houston that experience frequent coastal storms, Black and Latino residents are more likely to live in low-lying neighborhoods with a higher flood risk. Poor quality homes sustain greater damage from wind and water. Manufactured housing is one of the most affordable housing options in rural parts of the South and Midwest, and it provides the least protection against storms.[23] Within cities, low-income Black and brown neighborhoods have fewer trees and more asphalt, absorbing and holding in more heat in summer.[24] Racial discrimination in housing markets has limited Black and Latino families' access to greener, cooler, healthier neighborhoods.[25] The U.S. government systematically displaced Native Americans to some of the least desirable and most climate-vulnerable land. Blackfoot and Omaha reservations are subject to frequent flooding; high winds and tornados damage properties on Cherokee land; and the Pine Ridge reservation suffers from the effects of severe cold.[26]

Both financial resources and less tangible assets, like robust social networks, help people prepare for, avoid, and recover from extreme climate events.[27] It is easier to evacuate before a hurricane or approaching wildfire if you have money to pay for transportation and a hotel room somewhere safe. Disaster evacuation plans often assume that people can pile themselves and their belongings into a car and drive away, forgetting that poor people (especially in urban areas) are less likely to own a car. Low-income households, most of whom rent their homes, are much less likely to have insurance that reimburses them for damaged property. Generations of discriminatory policies have left Black, Latino, and Native communities with low levels of trust in public entities, which can translate into reluctance to follow official recommendations.[28]

Resource gaps at the community level affect the most essential outcomes: poor cities, counties, and territories often have higher casualty rates. Superstorm Sandy created tremendous physical and economic damage to the New York metro area—home to some of the wealthiest zip codes in the country—but had a relatively modest death toll, around 150 people.[29] More than 1,800 people died after Hurricane Katrina hit poor, largely Black, coastal areas in Louisiana and Mississippi. The official death count following Hurricane Maria was 2,975, but some estimates put it over 4,600.[30] Poor quality housing, roads and bridges, communications systems, backup power systems, the capacity to create safe shelters for those unable to evacuate—all these elements of disaster management require resources.

Like other forms of policy, community plans for climate risks and mitigation reflect power imbalances as well: who gets invited to sit at the table influences the content of the plans. Most middle-class Americans have air-conditioning in their homes, so they may not realize how deadly a summer heat wave can be for people without it.[31] To make public sector plans for climate adaptation and mitigation more effective, plans need to take into consideration the needs of socially and economically vulnerable residents.

Solutions

Building more homes in places with large household carbon footprints, or in places at high risk for climate-related harms, imposes large environmental, economic, and social costs. So why does so much housing get built in the wrong places? Broadly speaking, the problem is that the out-of-pocket costs paid by individual households are much lower than the costs borne by society at large (in economic jargon, there are unpriced externalities). Costs are distributed across a range of public and private institutions, including an alphabet soup of federal housing finance agencies and insurance programs. The system is complex and opaque, which makes it difficult for homeowners and taxpayers to understand who ultimately pays for climate damages. Untangling the overlapped strands will help policymakers design and implement more effective policy solutions.

*Homes in high-risk locations should be more expensive for buyers,
not taxpayers*

Let's start with the question of why people build (or buy) homes in places that are very likely to be affected by hurricanes, wildfires, rising sea levels, or all of the above. In many cases, the very attributes that make those locations risky also make them desirable to some home buyers. For people who want to enjoy oceanfront views or walks on the beach, proximity to the coast is a prized location—an amenity for which buyers are happy to pay a substantial premium. Sure, every ten years the house gets hit with a whopper of a storm, but in between, the lifestyle is lovely. And most coastal homeowners don't pay the full costs of repairing damage from storms and floods (more to follow on this issue). The same principle applies to some of the western areas at highest risk of wildfires. High-priced, low-density cities like La Canada-Flintridge and Malibu perch on hillsides with dramatic views of Los Angeles and the Pacific Ocean, but their proximity to adjacent forests puts them at high risk of wildfires.[32]

Amenity value isn't the only reason that people live in high-climate-risk locations, of course. For many low-income, Black or brown families, it's quite the opposite. Cheap housing can be found in low-lying neighborhoods with a persistent flood risk or in places where temperatures are rising every year. In some cities, these are the only neighborhoods that did not have legal barriers for nonwhite households in prior decades, so families put down roots, even knowing the risks.[33]

Long-standing property owners in high-risk places are stuck in a catch-22 situation. Once it becomes known that a neighborhood is likely to flood or burn, it becomes much harder for homeowners to sell their property and move somewhere safer. People who bought homes twenty years ago in what seemed then to be low-risk locations now face hurdles in moving—an issue that public policy acknowledges but hasn't allocated resources to solve.

Building homes in high-risk locations doesn't just impact the people who live there, it imposes costs on all of society. When disasters hit, emergency responders are sent into dangerous situations to protect residents and property. Their salaries and equipment, as well as some public insurance payouts, are paid for with local, state, and federal tax dollars. In effect, people who live in low-risk locations are subsidizing people in higher-risk zones. A more equitable and efficient system would require people to internalize the social harms of their choices, while providing support for those with few resources who want to move to lower-risk places.

Our complex system of mortgage and insurance markets divide financial risk among multiple parties, so that people who choose to buy homes in flood- and fire-prone areas bear only a small portion of the cost when things go wrong. A large chunk of the costs is borne by the federal government—that is to say, taxpayers—although the accounting is often hard to follow.

Consider a hypothetical home buyer who wanted to purchase a $250,000 home in Galveston, Texas, on the Gulf of Mexico. Few home buyers in the United States pay the full price in cash; the typical purchaser pays 10 to 15 percent up-front and borrows the remainder from a bank or other mortgage lender. Let's say our hypothetical home buyer bought the home in 2015, with 15 percent down. In 2017, Hurricane Harvey struck the Gulf Coast, flooding over 300,000 properties. If the house was damaged beyond repair, who would bear the financial costs (distinct from the emotional and physical impacts of living through a hurricane)? The homeowner had invested $37,500 in the initial down payment, and had likely built up a few thousand dollars additional equity over the two years. Leaving aside insurance for the moment (we'll return to this shortly), that leaves the mortgage lender with an outstanding loan amount slightly over $200,000, backed by a severely devalued asset.

But the lender probably isn't the ultimate loser in this scenario. Roughly two-thirds of U.S. mortgage loans are not retained on balance sheets by the originating lender.[34] Instead, the mortgages are sold to intermediaries who bundle them with other loans and sell the income stream to investors, a process called securitization. The largest two intermediaries, Fannie Mae and Freddie Mac, are government-sponsored enterprises (GSEs)—quasi-public companies that were originally chartered by the federal government. Under normal housing market conditions, Fannie and Freddie guarantee investors against the risk of borrowers defaulting. Investors who bought mortgage-backed securities issued by Fannie and Freddie implicitly believed that, if a housing crisis occurred that led to widespread mortgage defaults, the federal government would backstop their losses. The Great Recession saw exactly such an event. Since then, Fannie and Freddie are under federal conservatorship, meaning that they pay a portion of their profits into the U.S. Treasury, and are subject to supervision by Congress and the Federal Housing Finance Agency.[35]

The upshot of this complicated arrangement is that the federal government is essentially holding the bag on roughly $6.9 trillion of outstanding mortgage debt, including many properties in high-climate-risk locations.[36] Fannie and Freddie do require homeowners in designated flood-prone areas to purchase flood insurance (yet to be discussed), but the agencies do not take localized climate risk into account when securitizing loans.[37]

Climate risk could be priced into housing finance in several different ways. At the most stringent end, Fannie Mae and Freddie Mac could refuse to securitize mortgages on properties in high-risk locations. That would force originating lenders to consider whether they are willing to hold those mortgages on their balance sheet—and potentially absorb the losses. If home buyers could not obtain mortgages where climate risks are high, they could still choose to buy homes in those locations, but they would have to pay all cash—and thus assume the full risk of their decisions. A less drastic approach would be for Fannie and Freddie to continue securitizing loans in high-risk locations, but to incorporate climate risk into prices, through higher interest rates, lower loan-to-value ratios, or other fees. Implementing this would require the agencies to have frequently updated, geographically specific data on a wide range of climate risks—well beyond the flood maps currently used in federal

hazard mitigation.[38] Because the GSEs are currently under conservatorship, any changes in how they price climate risk would likely require
approval from Congress—politically not an easy task.[39]

*Climate insurance and disaster recovery programs should discourage risk and
mitigate racial disparities*

Let's circle back to the role of insurance in diffusing financial responsibility for climate risk. Most homeowners buy property insurance
through private, for-profit companies. (Having homeowner's insurance
is a requirement of obtaining a mortgage, so that lenders are financially
protected if something happens to the property.) However, the extent to
which insurance companies reimburse property owners after climate-
related disasters varies widely. While most policies cover damage from
wind, like trees falling through the roof, they generally don't protect
against flood damage—often the most expensive harm caused by hurricanes.[40] Nor do standard policies protect against earthquakes; homeowners can buy separate earthquake insurance, but even in California,
a minority of homeowners have chosen to do so.[41]

The federal government has become the primary source of insurance for flood damage through the earlier-mentioned NFIP. The NFIP
includes a complex set of programs. It maintains a set of maps that des-
ignate all parts of the United States according to their assessed risk level
and offers insurance policies to property owners, with premiums set
based on their "zones" in the flood maps. Property owners with federally
backed mortgages in designated special flood hazard areas (SFHAs) are
required to carry flood insurance, which in theory should help internalize the additional risk of choosing to live in high-risk locations. However, researchers have pointed out numerous problems with the NFIP,
including the accuracy and timeliness of the maps.[42] For instance, only
about 20 percent of properties in New York that were flooded during Superstorm Sandy had flood insurance, because the storm surge extended
well beyond the SFHA. Although flood risk is increasing in many locations due to climate change, insurance premiums under the NFIP adjust

slowly, so many homeowners are effectively paying premiums well below the actuarially fair price.

Two other federal programs play a critical role in climate adaptation specifically related to housing. Following large-scale climate events, the federal government provides financial assistance to property owners, business owners, and state and local governments through the Community Development Block Grant Disaster Recovery (CDBG-DR) Program. Unlike other types of CDBG funds, disaster recovery is not a recurring, formula-based program; it requires individual appropriations from Congress. Funds can be used for a wide range of purposes, including repair and rebuilding of permanent housing, demolition of damaged structures, and compensating property owners for losses. Researchers have raised several concerns with how CDBG-DR has been implemented, including encouraging property owners to rebuild in high-risk locations and providing less generous assistance to rental properties than homeowners.[43] Because each appropriation requires authorization from Congress, politics can determine the amount and speed of funding (e.g., Puerto Rico after Hurricane Maria).

Both CDBG-DR and the Federal Emergency Management Agency's Hazard Mitigation Grant Program provide funds for homeowners to sell flood-damaged or high-risk properties, in order to relocate to safer places. The federal government prohibits future rebuilding on properties acquired through these programs, generally setting them aside for open space. Demand to participate in both programs far exceeds available funding, suggesting the need for the federal government to speed up and scale up relocation of high-risk communities. Acquisition and relocation are particularly important options for low-income homeowners (and some small landlords) who are essentially trapped in their current location, with most of their wealth tied up in properties they cannot sell. Yet many of the groups who would most benefit from relocation have low levels of trust in the government, including low-income, elderly, Black, and Latino homeowners.[44]

As currently designed, federal housing finance and insurance sys-

tems do little to mitigate racial and economic inequities in exposure to
climate risk. Only about 40 percent of renter households have renters'
insurance that would reimburse them for personal property damage,
so they face larger financial losses in the event of disasters.[45] CDBG-DR
allocates more funds to homeowners than renters, despite the fact that
renters have lower incomes and wealth, and they are more likely to be
nonwhite.

One goal of federal climate policy should be to deter people from
buying homes in high-risk locations. Our current housing finance and
insurance programs make it nearly impossible for homeowners and taxpayers to understand who ultimately pays for climate damages—thereby
putting additional lives at risk.

*To shrink household carbon footprints, tax driving and legalize climate-friendly
land use*

There's a strong case to make that some locations with an especially
high risk of climate damage should be essentially off-limits to building
(or rebuilding) housing. The socially optimal strategy around dispersed,
low-density suburban growth is more complicated. Suburbs are not
an environmental problem per se; development patterns that increase
household carbon footprints are. To fix this, policy solutions should
tax environmentally harmful behaviors (like driving and energy use)
while lowering regulatory barriers that prohibit more climate friendly
land use patterns (small homes and mixed residential-commercial
neighborhoods).

Both policy and political rhetoric around suburban land use patterns
needs to acknowledge the economic forces underlying suburbanization. People and companies have been moving out of central cities for
nearly as long as the United States has existed, for two reasons.[46] First,
as people earn more income, they want to live in larger homes. Because
land is expensive near downtown, larger homes are cheaper to build outside the urban core. Second, the cost of moving people and goods has declined with technological improvements—from walking to horse-drawn

streetcars to electric streetcars to automobiles—allowing economic activity to spread out. Policies that try to push back directly against these economic forces are likely to fail, and will be political nonstarters.

A series of policy choices reinforce the market forces behind suburbanization, including several subsidies that make large suburban homes appear cheaper to households than their true social costs. These subsidies distort household location choices and exacerbate racial and economic disparities. As numerous researchers have detailed, the Federal Housing Administration's mortgage insurance program subsidized newly constructed suburban homes—primarily for white home buyers—while explicitly limiting mortgage availability in most urban neighborhoods.[47] Federal tax subsidies, such as the mortgage interest deduction, encourage affluent homeowners to buy more expensive homes with larger mortgages, an implicit bias toward suburban areas (discussed more in chapter 5). Mortgage lending rules penalize condominiums, which are mostly located in multifamily buildings.

Transportation subsidies also strongly influence the relative cost of living in cities versus suburbs. The development of the federal highway system from the 1950s through the 1970s substantially reduced the time needed to travel between downtown and suburban areas, enabling downtown workers to live at much greater distances from their employers—while undercutting economic demand and political support for central-city public transportation systems. Today, about 80 percent of revenues from the federal gas tax are allocated to maintenance of roads and highways—the dominant suburban transportation mode—with less than 20 percent set aside for public transit.[48]

As discussed in chapter 2, land use regulations play a substantial role in locking in low-density development patterns. In metro areas with a strong demand for centrally located neighborhoods, low-density zoning rules effectively suppress housing growth near downtown, pushing development out to car-dependent suburbs. Nudging affluent communities near Boston, New York, and San Francisco to relax their zoning must be part of the climate solution.

In metros like Baltimore and St. Louis, restrictive zoning is not the reason why little housing gets built downtown. The central cities in these metros have lost population since the mid-twentieth century. Manufacturing companies, which once anchored their downtowns, have moved out to the suburbs to be closer to highways and airports and have shed workers due to automation. In these metro areas, developers build most new homes in the suburbs because that is where most people—regardless of income and race—want to live. And because a larger share of employment is located in suburban job clusters, it is not clear that channeling population growth downtown would reduce the total amount of commuting, although it could encourage more efficient use of infrastructure (discussed in chapter 6).

Climate-friendly suburbs need to integrate housing, land use, and transportation

The built environment—homes, offices, stores, transportation networks—is extremely durable. Dismantling physical structures and spatial patterns that developed over many decades will not be quick or easy, even if we could wave a magic wand and align all the financial incentives correctly tomorrow. To start reshaping urban areas into more climate friendly places, we need to rebalance taxes and subsidies around transportation, create financial incentives for lower-carbon-footprint homes, and reform land use regulations to enable car-light lifestyles. Within this broad framework, the details of policies will vary across places, reflecting existing differences in where job clusters are located, land values, and transportation infrastructure. None of these policy changes would prohibit people from living in large, detached homes and driving their SUVs every day—but people who choose that lifestyle would have to shoulder the financial consequences.

Nudging people away from car-dependency and toward car-light lifestyles requires making driving more expensive and alternative transportation modes cheaper, easier, and more reliable. Exactly what that looks like will vary across metro areas and across neighborhoods. Dense urban centers with comparatively robust public transportation networks, like Manhattan and San Francisco, could use tools like congestion pricing to increase the cost of driving in the central business district during rush hour. Reducing the availability and increasing the cost of parking—for instance, converting on-street parking into dedicated bus or bike lanes and raising metered parking rates—would further encourage residents and workers to use noncar alternatives. Revenues raised from driving and parking can be invested in better public transportation, like more frequent bus service, and pedestrian infrastructure (sidewalks and crosswalks), creating a virtuous cycle.

Implementing a car-light lifestyle will look very different in metro areas like Houston and Detroit, where economic activity is thinly spread across enormous land area, and public transportation service is scarce (even more so outside metro areas). Taxing driving and parking if there are no reasonable alternatives just increases the financial burden on households, especially low-income workers who tend to live far from job clusters. In many metros and smaller towns, the most feasible way to improve public transportation is through a decidedly unsexy approach: better bus service. Designating part of existing roadways for dedicated bus lanes, purchasing electric buses, and hiring more drivers and support staff are much quicker and cheaper than building light rail or streetcar systems. Virtually every city, suburb, and small town in the United States would benefit from relatively inexpensive changes that make walking and cycling safer and more pleasant. These investments also have big equity payoffs: three groups who are least likely to drive include children, older adults, and low-income households.

Two types of land use changes will complement car-light lifestyles: removing barriers to smaller, denser homes and allowing mixed-use areas that integrate homes with jobs and services. These changes should be implemented in both suburban neighborhoods and the urban core.

In high-cost, supply constrained metro areas, relaxing zoning to allow more small homes on existing lots would enable more households to live within walking distance of job centers, shopping corridors, and public transit. Opponents of zoning reform often conjure "Manhattanization" as the feared outcome, as though any relaxation of current rules will result in high-rise buildings full of 150-square-foot studios. In reality, most places with restrictive zoning don't have sufficiently high land values to entice developers to build at such high density. Zoning changes that allow detached homes on smaller lots, rowhouses, duplexes, and low-rise multifamily buildings could add substantial amounts of housing and fit unobtrusively into most neighborhoods.

Finding ways to retrofit suburbia (a term coined by architect Ellen Dunham-Jones) is an important part of a climate-friendly future.[49] That is especially true in metro areas where a large share of jobs is located outside the traditional downtown. Places like Buckhead, Georgia; North Carolina's Research Triangle Park; and Itasca, Illinois, have large suburban office parks with an abundance of white-collar professional jobs, as well as retail, restaurants, and services. People who work in these clusters and live nearby can enjoy both cheaper housing and shorter commutes. Changing land use to encourage more housing within a short distance of suburban job clusters, and making the built environment more friendly to noncar transit of all types, is as important as focusing on the urban core. Sometimes these retrofits can work within the existing street grid; Colorado Boulevard in Pasadena, California, offers a good example. Developers are also building larger moderate-density, mixed-use projects that create new streets, public spaces, and related infrastructure, mimicking a traditional urban neighborhood but in a suburban setting. The Mosaic District in Fairfax, Virginia, and the Irvine Company's Spectrum Center in Orange County, California, are two examples.[50] Smaller-scale examples of mixed-use, pedestrian-oriented Main Streets are widely found across the United States, from Lancaster, Pennsylvania, to Covington, Kentucky.

Local governments have primary authority over land use regulation, but the federal government does have some policy levers to incentivize climate-friendly zoning changes. The federal insurance and disaster recovery programs described earlier could be redesigned to encourage communities to redirect housing development proactively, rather than focusing on rebuilding after disasters strike. Fannie Mae and Freddie Mac briefly experimented with location-efficient mortgages, offering discounted interest rates for homes near transit, on the grounds that reducing households' transportation costs would lower risk of mortgage default. In theory, the GSEs could incorporate climate friendliness into loan pricing, with lower interest rates based on a home's energy efficiency and proximity to jobs or transit. If the GSEs set price discounts for entire cities and counties, rather than at the property level, it could prove a substantial incentive for local governments to undertake zoning reforms.

Implicit in proposals for carbon taxes is that it will raise the price of energy used by both households and businesses, encouraging people to cut back on consumption (and switch to cleaner sources). Once again, how households make these lifestyle adjustments will vary across places. New homes are a small share of total housing, so it is likely that retrofitting existing homes will constitute a large part of the response. In slow population growth areas (metros in the Northeast and Midwest, rural areas), housing tends to be quite old and would benefit from energy-improving upgrades to windows and doors, or installing more insulation.[51] To avoid creating undue cost burdens on low-income homeowners through higher utility costs, federal and state governments should expand existing programs that offer low-interest loans or grants, such as the U.S. Department of Energy's Weatherization Assistance Program.[52] The unusual winter storms that hit Texas and Louisiana in February 2021 illustrate that even Sunbelt metros—which have relatively new housing—will need upgrades and adjustments in response to climate change.

Conclusion

The United States' current approach to climate change is unsustainable in every possible way. In coming years, climate change will wreak even more havoc on households and communities than it has to date. U.S. taxpayers are already absorbing the costs, although often through convoluted and opaque mechanisms that make full accounting difficult. Current policies, from federal housing finance and transportation to local zoning and building codes, create misaligned incentives, encouraging risky and harmful behavior by individual households and communities who do not bear the full social costs of their actions. Costs of both acute and chronic climate change are disproportionately borne by low-income, Black and brown households, compounding the harms from decades of overt discrimination. National policy debates about climate change have traditionally ignored housing, land use, and transportation—but aligning these policy areas will be critical to achieving effective and equitable solutions.

4

Give Poor People Money

Bad things happen sometimes. Over the course of a lifetime, most of us will have unexpected experiences that harm our economic well-being. Events such as serious illness or injury, natural disasters, or recessions can happen to anyone at almost any time, causing at least temporary loss of income. Social insurance programs exist to catch people when such events happen, to make sure that people can continue to receive medical care and put food on the table. Food stamps, Medicaid, Social Security, and unemployment insurance are examples of social insurance programs.[1] Crucially, all these examples are entitlement programs: all persons or households who meet certain eligibility criteria (usually based on income or work status) are entitled to receive benefits, regardless of how many other people are already receiving benefits.

Housing is the largest single budget item for most low- and moderate-income families. Keeping a roof over one's head is just as important as being able to buy food and receive health care. Yet, in contrast to food stamps and Medicaid, housing assistance for low-income households is not an entitlement. Rather, Congress allocates a pot of funds (really, several different pots) that can be distributed to households until the money runs out. About one in four eligible low-income households receives federal housing assistance at any given time.[2] Many poor households who qualify for benefits will never receive them because the queue ahead of them is too long.

Even if we could remove all regulatory barriers to well-functioning housing markets, the cost of market-rate housing would still be too high for some people and families to afford. In 2019, more than 10 million renters spent over half their income on rent—an unsustainable expense that leaves them vulnerable to displacement. Ensuring that everyone in the United States has access to decent quality, stable housing would make the United States a safer, healthier, more productive place for everyone.

Poor families face a gap between their incomes and housing costs

As any homeowner can attest, keeping a home in good condition isn't cheap. The same principles apply to operating and maintaining rental housing. Most apartment buildings have mortgages, just as owner-occupied homes do. Every month, landlords have to pay their lenders principal and interest on the mortgage. Then there are property taxes owed to the local government and annual premiums on insurance policies. For most rental properties, the landlord also covers payments for some utilities, such as water and sewer bills, trash and recycling pickup, heating, cooling, and electricity for common areas like hallways. Depending on the size of the building, there may be on-site maintenance and housekeeping staff, whose salaries have to be paid, or bills to independent contractors to provide those services. Elevators have to be maintained in working condition. Roofs leak. Pipes break. Grass needs mowing. Snow has to be shoveled. Even if landlords perform some of these tasks themselves, they have to buy materials and equipment. Just as homeowners occasionally face big-ticket expenses—replacing the water heater or air-conditioning—property owners have to set aside funds into a reserve account for capital expenses.

The costs of operating and maintaining rental housing create an effective floor for rents. Like any other business, if landlords cannot charge monthly rents that cover their operating costs, then they have to close down, either selling the property or simply letting the building sit vacant. Even not-for-profit organizations that operate rental housing have to collect enough income to keep the mortgage paid and the lights on. In practice, it is nearly impossible to operate rental housing that meets minimum health and safety requirements for less than $500 per month.[3]

Which raises the question: are there people who can't afford to spend $500 each month on rent?

How much income people can—or should—spend on housing costs, relative to their other expenses, is not a simple question. The U.S. Department of Housing and Urban Development uses a standard benchmark: households who spend more than 30 percent of their monthly income on housing (including utilities) are deemed "cost burdened," while those who spend more than 50 percent are "severely cost-burdened."[4] This implies that to afford $500 per month for rent, a household would need an annual income of around $20,000.

While the 30 percent benchmark is widely used, economists point out that it doesn't take into account differences across households in preferences and resources. Is a household spending 31 percent of income really that much worse off than a similar family spending 29 percent? What if some people choose to spend more money to rent an apartment close to their job, which allows them to avoid the expenses of owning a car? Or a family that is willing to scrimp on other costs in order to move their children into a better school district? What about someone with a monthly student debt payment that eats up 15 percent of their income—can they still afford to pay 30 percent for housing?

An alternative approach to measuring affordability is to determine how much cash a household will have left over after paying for housing, and assess whether they can still afford other necessities, like food, transportation, clothes, and health care. This "residual income" approach can be adjusted for family size and local differences in cost of living. As of 2015, renters in the poorest 20 percent of households earned around $1,100 per month and paid about $600 each month in rent, leaving less than $500 to cover other expenses (figure 4-1). According to the federal government's Supplemental Poverty Measure, a family of four would need about $1,400 per month to pay for nonhousing expenses— nearly three times as much cash as they had.

Using either the typical housing cost burden approach or the residual income approach tells the same story: the poorest 20 percent of U.S. households simply don't have enough income to pay for market-rate housing. This is true for households in big cities, small towns, and rural areas, and in all regions of the country. Families with children are particularly squeezed by housing costs, in part because they have higher expenses per wage-earning adult (table 4-1).[5] And many of these households are working full-time jobs, but for very low wages.[6]

FIGURE 4-1. Low-income renters have little cash left after paying rent. *Residual income, by income quintile (%).*

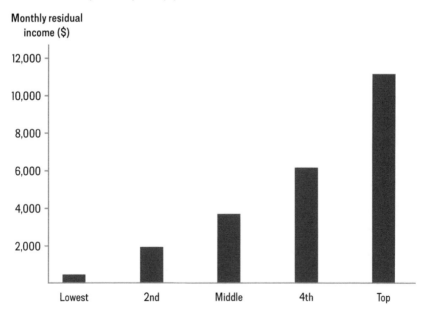

Source: Jeff Larrimore and Jenny Schuetz, "Assessing the Severity of Rent Burden on Low Income Families," Board of Governors of the Federal Reserve System, FEDS Notes, December 22, 2017.

TABLE 4-1. Low-income families with children and renters of all races face heavy rent burdens.

	RENT/INCOME	INCOME AFTER RENT ($)	SHARE WHO RENT (%)
Family structure			
With kids < 18 yrs	0.60	443	73
Head 65+	0.44	593	38
Race and Ethnicity			
White	0.55	496	48
Black	0.54	454	74
Asian	0.78	250	65
Hispanic	0.57	496	72

Source: Jeff Larrimore and Jenny Schuetz, "Assessing the Severity of Rent Burden on Low Income Families," Board of Governors of the Federal Reserve System, FEDS Note, December 22, 2017.

Note: Median values in 2015 for the lowest income quintile, defined by local income. Income remaining after rent is expressed monthly.

In short, housing affordability for poor families isn't the same problem created by tight zoning regulations in cities like New York and San Francisco. Millions of families across the United States cannot afford housing because their incomes are too low—a problem that implies different types of policy solutions.

How the other quintile lives

Choosing a home means selecting a complicated bundle of options: the physical quality and size of a home, proximity to work or school, neighborhood amenities like parks and school quality, and of course the monthly cost. Households trying to save money on housing can adjust their behavior along several different dimensions. They can move into a smaller living space ("downsizing") or accept lower-quality housing. Neighborhoods with fewer amenities—far from job centers, with fewer stores or higher crime rates—generally offer cheaper rents. For middle-income households, economizing on housing might mean moving from a two-bedroom to a one-bedroom apartment, or putting up with a longer commute to work. But for poor households, nearly all the options they can afford are unpleasant, uncomfortable, or unsafe.

Renters spending a large share of their monthly income on housing are at high risk of housing instability and displacement. In order to pay their rent, families often fall behind on other bills, such as utilities, car payments, or credit cards. Ethnographic research details how families juggle competing financial obligations, skipping rent one month to pay the electric bill or cell phone, until the landlord's patience runs out. For many poor households with overstretched budgets, falling behind on rent is inevitable, leading to evictions or involuntary moves.[7] Low-income renters change addresses more frequently than higher-income households, a pattern that imposes financial and emotional costs, especially on children.[8]

One common strategy to stretch a tight housing budget is "doubling-up," sharing one house or apartment with multiple families. The U.S. Department of Housing and Urban Development (HUD) defines any household with more than two persons per bedroom as crowded. Nationally, only 3 percent of U.S. households are crowded. But among low- and moderate-income families with children living in expensive metros, that number is around 15 percent.[9] Overcrowding is especially prevalent among Latino families in high-cost markets like California; it is not uncommon to find ten people—adults and children—belonging to three unrelated families sharing one home.[10] As of 2000, over half the children in Los Angeles County lived in overcrowded homes.[11]

Families trying to economize on rent often end up in poor quality housing—sometimes below the minimum guidelines set by building and health code regulations. This is not a new problem. In the nineteenth century, Jacob Riis shocked middle-class Americans with his photos of unsanitary, overcrowded tenement housing in New York City. Lyndon Johnson's War on Poverty in the 1960s revealed poor quality housing across rural areas, including many homes that still lacked indoor plumbing and electricity.[12] Nearly all homes in the United States today have these basic features—with the notable exception of Native Americans living on tribal lands.[13] Typical housing quality problems today are more nuanced and are not well measured by official data sources. Persistent maintenance problems—leaky plumbing, malfunctioning heating systems, hazardous materials such as lead paint and asbestos—are still present, especially in older homes.[14] Infestations of rodents or insects left unmitigated create health hazards, especially to children with asthma and other respiratory problems. Living in poor quality housing is not uniquely a problem for renters, or a malevolent choice by landlords. Many low-income homeowners living in older homes face similar problems, but they lack the resources to fix them.

Some people live in unregulated informal housing—buildings that are not licensed or approved for residential use. Informal housing often comes to light when tragedy hits, such as recent fires in the Ghost Ship warehouse in Oakland and an illegal rowhouse sublet in Washington, DC.[15] Counting how many people live in unregulated housing is nearly impossible, since neither building owners nor tenants want to alert government officials to the arrangement.

In extreme circumstances, people become homeless, meaning they have no fixed place to live. Every January, HUD conducts a point-in-time count of homeless people across the U.S, sending thousands of volunteers and staff out to tally people.[16] They count people staying in homeless shelters, as well as unsheltered people sleeping on sidewalks, parks and other public spaces, and highway and train underpasses. In 2020, the point-in-time count estimated roughly 580,000 homeless people, just under 40 percent of whom were unsheltered.[17] California has the largest homeless population in the United States and one of the highest rates of unsheltered households. High-cost metros like the Bay Area have seen increasing numbers of families with children—many of them with jobs but unable to afford rent—living in cars and recreational vehicles.

In describing housing distress, researchers and policymakers focus much more on cost burdens than on housing quality or crowding. Severe cost burdens are a more widespread problem: nationally about 60 percent of unassisted poor households spend more than half their income on rent.[18] But housing quality also tends to draw less attention because it is more difficult to measure accurately with available data. The most frequently used public dataset, the American Community Survey, does not capture relevant housing quality issues. The American Housing Survey, jointly sponsored by the Census Bureau and HUD, has much more detailed questions on both structural housing problems and maintenance concerns. In 2017, about 550,000 low-income renter households had severely inadequate housing. But the incidence of poor-quality housing is higher among certain population groups: single mothers with children are most likely to live in inadequate housing.[19] Older housing is especially prevalent in the Midwest and Northeast; more than 80 percent of low- and moderate-income households in Cleveland live in older homes with high maintenance needs, shown in figure 4-2.[20]

Lack of decent quality, stable housing doesn't just harm poor families

In his second inaugural address, President Franklin Roosevelt famously pointed to "one-third of a nation ill-housed, ill-clad, ill-nourished." He did so as a call to action, stating his hope that "because the nation, seeing and understanding the injustice in [this picture], proposes to paint it out."[21] Relying on the public spirit and altruism of more affluent citizens may or may not be enough to motivate voters and policymakers to develop a stronger safety net. But we don't need to rely on altruism alone. The lack of decent quality, stable housing creates substantial costs on the broader society—costs to public health and safety, worker productivity, and investment in future generations.

The COVID-19 pandemic has drawn renewed attention to the public health dangers associated with poor quality and overcrowded housing. Nineteenth-century tenement reformers were acutely aware of how

FIGURE 4-2. Lower-income households occupy older, poorer-quality homes.
Share of households in 50+ year-old homes by metro.

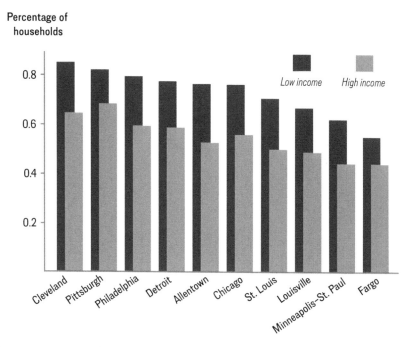

Source: Steven Ruggles, Sarah Flood, Sophia Foster, Ronald Goeken, Jose Pacas, Megan Schouweiler, and Matthew Sobek. IPUMS USA: Version 11.0 (dataset), IPUMS, 2021, https://doi.org/10.18128/D010.V11.0.

overcrowding threatened public health: contagious diseases spread more rapidly when people lived in close proximity to one another, lacking adequate facilities for hygiene and personal space.[22] The same is true today: community transmission rates of COVID-19 are higher in areas with more crowded housing—not places with higher population density.[23] Housing instability also poses risks during contagious disease outbreaks. Families that are evicted or otherwise displaced necessarily move somewhere else, increasing the number of new contacts they are exposed to. Indeed, the Centers for Disease Control and Prevention invoked public health concerns to impose a nationwide eviction moratorium.[24]

From a social perspective, the highest costs associated with poor housing quality and instability are the impacts on children's well-being and development. Children who grow up in homes with environmental toxins, such as lead paint or mold, suffer both short-term health problems (asthma attacks) and longer-term behavioral and developmental problems.[25] Living in an overcrowded home is particularly harmful for young children, because they spend most of their time at home. Too little space shared by too many people—and the stress that imposes on parents and children—impedes children's ability to study, sleep, and socialize.[26] As discussed in chapter 2, the neighborhoods where children grow up are also critically important to their lifetime educational achievements and income. Families rarely *choose* to live in unsafe neighborhoods with underperforming schools; rather, they cannot afford better options.

If the United States wants to have a healthy, well-educated, productive workforce twenty years from now, then investing in better-quality living environments for children today is not merely an act of compassion but an economic necessity.

To solve the problem of low incomes, give poor people more money

The most direct, straightforward way to help poor people pay for decent-quality housing is to give them more money. Outside coastal cities, housing cost burdens are primarily the result of low incomes, rather than insufficient housing, so the solution is simply to raise incomes.

As with any income transfer program, there are several critical policy design questions to be addressed. First, which level of government should provide funding? Second, how much money should each person or family receive? Third, can the program be designed to minimize unintended consequences, such as reducing people's incentive to work or encouraging landlords to raise rents?

Income transfers and other antipoverty programs are most effectively funded by the federal government, rather than by state and local governments. The logic for this is simple: if some cities or states decided to offer relatively generous income supplements to poor people, compared with neighboring cities or states, then poor people would choose to move to the most generous jurisdiction—which would then be overwhelmed by demand. By moving responsibility for income transfers to the federal government, we avoid the "fly-paper effect." Moreover, the cities and states with the fewest resources—lower-income residents, fewer businesses, lower-value properties—have both the greatest need for assistance and the least ability to provide aid. That discrepancy becomes especially large during recessions, when state and local government revenue sources dry up and demand spikes. As discussed in chapter 6, state and local governments face more institutional constraints on their ability to borrow and to raise revenues than the federal government.

The federal government already has several existing programs that supplement incomes for people at the lower end of the income distribution. Expanding one or more of these would be an administratively easy way to get more money to poor people for housing. The largest program, the earned income tax credit (EITC), is a federal tax credit for low- and moderate-income working families.[27] Only households that earn some income through paid employment are eligible (designed to incentivize work). Families with children receive more generous credits, although working adults with no dependent children can receive a small credit. Research has shown that the EITC is effective at increasing maternal employment and reducing poverty rates for families with children.[28]

The federal child tax credit (CTC) provides up to $2,000 per child for qualifying families. Prior to 2021, the CTC was not fully refundable, meaning that many low-earning families received less than the maximum amount.[29] The American Recovery Act adopted in March 2021 temporarily increased the amount of the CTC to $3,000 and made it fully refundable, changes that are predicted to lift 4.1 million children above the poverty line.[30] The EITC and CTC have traditionally had more bipartisan support than some of the low-income housing subsidies administered through HUD.

There is one substantial disadvantage of relying on the EITC—or most programs administered through the federal tax system—to help poor families pay for housing. Rent is due every month, but the EITC is paid out to families once a year when they file their federal tax returns. Qualitative research has shown that families do rely on the EITC to cover housing costs.[31] Families who expect to receive the EITC in April may choose to prioritize other expenses over rent in the months leading up to April, falling behind on their rent, then pay off some accumulated rent debt once their EITC check comes through. But they run the risk that landlords move forward with eviction proceedings in the meantime. Arranging for EITC checks to be sent out monthly or quarterly could improve low-income families' housing security even without expanding the size of benefits, although it would be administratively more complicated.[32]

Aside from tax policies, the federal government has another existing tool to increase incomes: the federal minimum wage. Currently set at $7.25 per hour, Congress has not chosen to raise the minimum wage since 2007, although twenty-nine states and the District of Columbia have adopted higher payment standards.[33] While increasing the federal minimum wage would likely make it easier for some low-income families to pay for housing, this would be a less precisely targeted mechanism, even if there were no off-setting job losses. Millions of families with high housing cost burdens live in states that already exceed the federal minimum wage, including some of the largest and most expensive states, such as California, Massachusetts, and New York.

An alternative type of income transfer that has received increasing attention—most notably from 2020 Democratic presidential candidate Andrew Yang—is a universal basic income (UBI). UBI programs can be structured in a variety of ways, but they are generally conceived of as payments from the government to a broad swath of the population rather than a targeted segment (hence, "universal") and would be large enough to cover minimum ("basic") living expenses.[34] A major sticking point in academic and policy debates is whether a UBI would *supplement* existing income transfer programs, including EITC, food stamps, and housing assistance, or would *replace* them. This issue is important both in estimating the total cost of any potential program and whether it would make low-income households better or worse off than they are now.

To date, the United States has not yet tried a large-scale UBI. Private donors funded a small pilot program in Stockton, California, starting in 2019. The city randomly selected 125 households to receive $500 per month for two years with no strings attached (no work requirements). Early evidence suggests that the program did not discourage participants from working, and participants reported improved financial, physical, and emotional well-being.[35] It is still too early to predict whether the apparently positive outcomes in Stockton might result in other experimental programs on a larger scale.

One potential limitation of trying to address housing security though federal income supplements is the need to incorporate geographic differences. Housing costs vary widely across regions of the country. Programs like the EITC, CTC, Social Security, and even food stamps, are not designed to adjust benefit levels by geography—unlike virtually all the federal housing subsidy programs discussed in the next section. Incorporating geographic variation in tax credits is theoretically possible, but it raises some additional challenges. Further, increasing income supplements to many poor families in regions of the country where housing supply is constrained by local regulatory barriers may be counterproductive: landlords could raise rents accordingly, leaving families no better off.[36]

Better functioning, more flexible housing markets are necessary but not sufficient

Reforming zoning laws, building codes, and other regulations to streamline the housing production system are essential to achieving any meaningful reduction in housing costs. But we should also be realistic about whether better-functioning housing markets would enable low-income households to afford decent-quality housing without subsidy. Newly built housing has rarely (if ever) been affordable to low-income households. Building enough new housing to satisfy demand for middle- and higher-income households would ease some pressure on poor families, because they would face less competition for older, existing homes, which could "filter down" in cost, as discussed in chapter 2.

Three types of regulatory reforms would be particularly helpful to low- and moderate-income households. First, relax zoning restrictions on housing density, such as prohibitions on multifamily buildings and minimum lot/unit sizes. It is impossible to build subsidized apartments, such as low-income housing tax credit (LIHTC) projects, in places where local zoning prohibits multifamily structures. Recipients of federal housing vouchers can only rent apartments in neighborhoods that have suitably priced rental housing. In places where land costs are high, the easiest way to reduce per-unit housing costs is to build more homes on a single land parcel. Stacking small apartments vertically, even in relatively low rise buildings, can substantially lower the per-unit cost of each home. Allowing existing single-family homes to be subdivided into multiple small apartments—a process that already occurs, often illegally—should also be a priority for local governments concerned about affordability.

Second, rethink building codes that require full kitchens and separate bathrooms for every household. The expectation that each person or nuclear family must have a completely equipped kitchen and bath is relatively recent in human history. In the nineteenth and early twentieth centuries, low-wage workers had a wider range of cheap, shared housing options, including boarding houses with shared bathrooms and communal dining halls, worker dormitories, and single-room occupancy hotels.[37] Today these structures and living arrangements are prohibited by a whole network of regulations, including zoning laws, building codes, and occupancy requirements. Re-legalizing them would expand housing options to low-income people, and remove the threat of sanction from property owners who offer similar homes for rent.

Third, remove regulatory barriers to manufactured and modular housing. Manufactured housing offers substantial cost savings over traditional "stick-built" homes in places where land costs are relatively low, because it reduces the construction labor and materials costs. This would be especially helpful in rural areas or cities with a high incidence of vacant lots, such as Detroit or Baltimore.

Better-functioning housing markets would also improve the efficacy of HUD's largest (by number of recipients) subsidy program: housing vouchers. Vouchers allow low-income households to rent an apartment from a private landlord, with the federal government picking up most of the rental tab. Households spend 30 percent of their income on rent, while the remainder—up to a designated Fair Market Rent—is covered by HUD. Vouchers are a relatively straightforward way to supplement poor families' ability to pay for housing and have proven to be effective at reducing housing instability.[38]

The biggest limitation of the voucher program is that, because it is not an entitlement, the number of vouchers that Congress has chosen to fund is not nearly enough to cover all poor families. The shortage of vouchers is an entirely fixable problem: it just requires money and political will. Put into international context, most other wealthy countries offer some type of rental assistance similar to vouchers, but as an entitlement, so that all eligible households receive help.[39]

That is not to say there isn't room for improvement within the voucher program.[40] Some families offered vouchers are unable to find available apartments that meet HUD's rent and quality requirements in the time allotted to them. In most parts of the United States, landlords are not required to accept vouchers as a form of payment. Recent research has indicated that a variety of technical fixes could increase landlords' acceptance, including targeted outreach from housing authorities and offering security deposits backed by the local administering agency.[41] In states that have passed source of income discrimination laws, landlords are prohibited from refusing to accept vouchers—although these laws are less effective in tight housing markets when landlords have multiple applicants for an apartment. To make it easier for voucher holders to rent homes in high-opportunity neighborhoods, which typically have more expensive housing, HUD has experimented with varying the maximum payment standard across zip codes, known as Small Area Fair Market Rents.[42] The cost of these improvements is small relative to the direct rental subsidy, while having the potential to greatly increase long-run social returns through providing families with better-quality housing and neighborhoods.

While federal rental subsidies typically focus on households with long-term financial challenges, the COVID-19 pandemic has illustrated the need for more short-term emergency rental assistance. When local or regional job markets collapse, there is often a sudden spike in households that cannot cover their rent or mortgage for a period of weeks or months. One solution would be for the federal government to provide block grants to state or local governments for short-term emergency rental assistance programs, similar to those used after natural disasters. Tying these block grants to indicators of local economic distress, such as state or metro area unemployment rates, would simplify the need for Congress to vote on urgent one-off situations.[43]

Market-based approaches won't solve housing problems for everyone

Since the 1970s, federal housing subsidies in the United States have largely shifted toward decentralized, household-based, more market-oriented programs like vouchers, and away from traditional "project-based" subsidies, notably public housing.[44] The inventory of public housing—apartments built with federal subsidies, owned and operated by public agencies—has been declining since the mid-1990s, when a series of policies encouraged redevelopment of large, financially and physically distressed public housing complexes.[45] The largest affordable housing production program today, LIHTC, is funded through federal income tax credits, and is built, owned, and managed by a network of for-profit and nonprofit developers. Both Democratic and Republican presidents have largely supported this policy shift. Construction subsidies are more expensive per housing unit than housing vouchers, especially in restrictively zoned places; in California, developing a new LIHTC project costs $480,000 per unit.[46] Congress hasn't provided adequate long-term funding for capital needs and maintenance of existing public housing properties (regardless of which party controls it), which puts local housing authorities in a difficult position. Even nonprofit organizations who own LIHTC or other subsidized rental properties have to raise additional funds for periodic capital upgrades (new LIHTC projects are required to remain affordable for at least thirty years).

Which raises the question as to whether there is still an argument in favor of federal subsidies to construct, own, and operate designated below-market housing. Put another way, in an alternative universe, where housing markets were allowed to produce lots of housing in the right places without undue regulatory burdens, and all poor families received either cash transfers or vouchers, would there still be people who lacked access to decent-quality, stable housing? (Given the decades-long deficit in housing construction in many parts of the country and the limited appetite for expanding subsidies, asking this question is largely a thought exercise.)

The clearest case to be made for public or nonprofit ownership of subsidized properties is that some people require more than just an apartment and a voucher to remain safely housed. For people with chronic mental or physical health problems, just being provided with cash or a voucher and directed to find an apartment isn't sufficient: they also need a range of supportive services in an appropriate environment.[47] A large and growing number of older adults need help with activities of daily living, such as eating, bathing, and dressing, or instrumental activities of daily living, such as managing medications or grocery shopping. While some privately funded, market-based housing providers do offer a combination of housing and services for older adults (typically called "assisted living"), these facilities are expensive, well beyond the means of most middle-income families, let alone poor Americans. Housing subsidies such as vouchers are not designed to cover the additional cost of meals and services, any more than health care subsidies are intended to pay for rent.[48] Supportive housing for older adults, and for people of all ages with special needs, requires a different model of financial subsidy and lends itself more easily to mission-driven not-for-profit ownership and management.

Beyond supportive housing, there are some local housing markets where maintaining a stock of non–privately owned apartments is probably a necessary bulwark. Places like New York City and San Francisco have accumulated a thirty-year housing deficit, combined with extraordinarily high land values that reflect their labor market productivity. Private property owners who want to maximize the returns on their investment have both the incentive and the ability to charge very high rents on residential apartments. In these types of housing markets, there's a strong social welfare argument for some housing being owned by public or nonprofit entities that are willing to keep rents close to operating costs over time, even as land values rise. Local labor markets function better when housekeepers and baristas and grocery store workers can live within reasonable proximity of their jobs, even though those workers will never be able to compete for housing against hedge fund managers and technology magnates.

While public housing in the United States has at best a mixed record, other wealthy countries have developed and operated public housing that serves a much wider segment of the rental market. More than 40 percent of renter households in France live in public housing, including many middle-income renters.[49] Nearly 80 percent of all housing in Singapore is built by the central government, which sells apartments to income-eligible households at below-market prices.[50] Two-thirds of Vienna's housing falls under some form of rent regulation, including public housing owned by the municipality, limited-equity cooperatives, and privately owned rent-regulated apartments.[51] U.S. housing policy could certainly benefit from more study of practices in other countries. But these different policies have emerged from each country's unique history, financial and legal institutions, and political context; importing good ideas from abroad will be more complicated than a straight copy-paste approach.

Vulnerable renters need more consistent legal protection

In recent years, sociologists and journalists have drawn attention to a difficult-to-quantify challenge facing low-income renters: some landlords engage in unethical abusive behavior, such as refusing to fix maintenance problems and harassing or threatening tenants.[52] The solutions already discussed—giving poor people enough money so that they can walk away from poor-quality homes and abusive landlords—would help somewhat. But rent subsidies alone will not address the power imbalance that enables exploitive or abusive behavior, especially toward vulnerable renter groups, including undocumented immigrants and returning citizens.

Landlord-tenant laws are adopted at the state level, so there is wide variation in what legal protections tenants are supposed to have—and the extent to which laws are enforced. Most other developed countries regulate leases and tenant protections at the federal level, which provides greater consistency and transparency. Chapter 8 considers how renter protections could be incorporated into federal oversight. More state or federal resources for legal aid could help with enforcement of current tenant protections. Tenant advocates have proposed a number of changes to the legal framework around evictions, including guaranteeing a right to counsel. However, laws that make it very difficult for landlords to remove problematic tenants have the potential to backfire, encouraging landlords to "screen" out less desirable renters up-front.[53] The experience of other countries provides some evidence that overly strong tenant protections can deter property owners from becoming landlords, leading to a smaller rental housing stock.[54] Finding the right balance between protecting vulnerable renters while still encouraging a healthy rental market can be tricky.

Conclusion

Decent-quality, healthy, stable housing is an essential human need. Even in well-functioning housing markets, poor households—especially families with children—cannot afford to pay rent equivalent to the operating costs of minimum-quality housing. All of society benefits from enabling children to grow up in high-opportunity neighborhoods, in families without undue financial stress. The federal government already has several mechanisms to give poor families more money, from refundable tax credits to housing vouchers. Expanding the funding available for these subsidies, paired with reduced regulatory barriers, would greatly improve living conditions for millions of low-income people. Economic self-interest and basic human compassion make these investments a no-brainer.

5

Homeownership Should Be Only
One Component of Household Wealth

Wealth creates a financial cushion for households, an additional measure of security. As the COVID-19 pandemic has vividly shown, having enough assets set aside to cover basic needs for a few months can allow families to stay sheltered, fed, and safe during an economic downturn. It enables people to meet unexpected expenses, like health emergencies or car repairs, without having to sacrifice current needs. And it allows households to plan for and invest in their future: sending children to college, starting a small business, retiring from full-time work.

For most middle-income Americans, the equity accumulated in their homes is the largest single source of wealth (figure 5-1). Homeownership has been marketed as a cornerstone of the American lifestyle, as a source of both individual wealth-building and community stability. But there are substantial downsides—for families and for the nation—to relying on homeownership as the primary strategy for accumulating wealth. For individuals and households, putting all their savings into a single asset is financially risky. Decades of discrimination in housing and mortgage markets have limited Black and Latino households from be-

FIGURE 5-1. Home equity is the largest wealth source for
middle-income households.
Homeownership rates and home equity as percent of wealth, by income quintile.

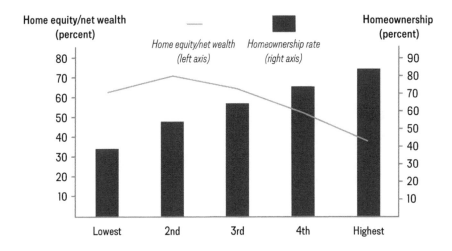

Source: U.S. Census Bureau, Survey of Income and Program Participation (2015).

coming homeowners, contributing to persistent racial wealth gaps. Current homeownership subsidies in the federal income tax code are highly
regressive, with the largest benefits accruing to affluent households.

A more balanced approach to wealth-building should redesign existing homeownership subsidies to better target first-time homeowners,
while also encouraging short-term and long-term wealth-building outside homeownership.

Homeownership can be an effective tool for accumulating wealth

Owning a home is one of the oldest and most common ways to build
wealth. Much of the appeal lies in the fact that housing is both a consumption good—everyone needs a place to live—and a financial asset
that can appreciate over time (unlike microwave ovens and computers).

You can either spend your monthly housing budget building equity for yourself or paying rent to some distant landlord. It is worth unpacking how owning a home can create wealth, so that we can apply some of these lessons to other forms of asset building.

One reason why buying a home is a great deal, relative to other asset types, is because of federal policy choices. Almost no one in the United States buys their home outright. Homes are too expensive for most households to purchase with cash. Over the twentieth century, the U.S. government devoted considerable thought and resources to designing, creating, and supporting a national mortgage market with the express goal of providing inexpensive loans to home buyers.[1] Because of implicit subsidies through the government-sponsored enterprises, Fannie Mae and Freddie Mac, mortgage markets offer cheaper interest rates than other types of consumer debt, like auto loans and credit cards.[2] Home buyers in the United States can buy a home while paying less than 10 percent of the purchase price up front, financing the remainder through a thirty-year fixed-rate mortgage, at prime interest rates that have been below 6 percent since the Great Recession.[3] Try buying stocks or mutual funds for your IRA on the same terms.

The type of mortgage commonly used to finance homes in the United States—a fully amortizing, thirty-year fixed-rate mortgage—also explains why homeownership is a simple and effective way to build wealth. Borrowers pay the same dollar amount every month for the duration of the loan. Some portion of the payment covers interest, the remainder accrues to equity ("pays down" the loan balance). In early years, most of the monthly payment goes toward interest, so equity accrues slowly, but the share of principal increases slightly each month. Home buyers don't need to make a conscious decision each month to set aside money in a savings account or retirement plan—just paying their monthly mortgage creates a pot of savings. This forced savings mechanism is one of the most effective ways to combat human nature's tendency to prefer spending money today over saving for tomorrow—a useful tool to remember when we consider alternate wealth-building strategies.[4]

The forced savings mechanism helps the homeowner accumulate wealth even if the house does not substantially increase in value. If housing prices rise at the rate of overall inflation, homeowners won't necessarily wind up richer than nonowners who put an equivalent amount of money each month into the S&P 500 index fund, for instance. But a third channel through which homeownership can create wealth depends on how much housing costs (both rents and prices) increase over time. Obviously, buying a home in a location that sees large increases in value will make homeownership a better investment than buying in a slower-growth location. Additionally, buying a home serves as a hedge against rents rising faster than income.[5] That is, a homeowner who takes on a thirty-year fixed-rate mortgage has a high degree of certainty about what their housing costs will be over a long period of time. (Property taxes and homeowner's insurance costs can rise, but these are usually small compared to principal and interest payments.) Renters in the United States typically sign a lease that lasts for only one year, with no guarantee of what the landlord will charge when the lease expires. The fact that renters face higher uncertainty about future housing costs is itself a function of policy choices and looks different in other countries.[6]

Summing up, homeownership allows households to borrow cheaply to leverage their initial investment and build wealth over time through forced savings, and it provides a hedge against future rent increases. With all these advantages, why shouldn't people go all in on homeownership?

Putting all one's financial eggs into the homeownership basket is risky

Homeownership breaks one of the key rules of finance: diversification. Financial planners recommend that clients spread their stock portfolio across a range of companies and industries, such as an index fund, rather than putting all their money into a single company.[7] Even if General Motors or Google stock performs poorly in some years, the remaining 498 companies in the S&P 500 probably won't. Buying a home is the opposite of diversification: it concentrates a person's resources in a single physical asset, industry, and location. And because most people's homes are located near where they work, homeownership commits another financial sin: returns to homeownership are positively correlated with returns to employment. That is, the likelihood that your house appreciates in value over time mirrors the health of labor markets in your city or region. This correlation implies that homeownership can create big winners—and big losers.

Housing prices are not guaranteed to increase over time, or even to match the rate of inflation. Across the United States, housing price appreciation has varied tremendously over the past forty years. A family that bought the median home in the city of Cleveland in 1980 would have paid roughly $86,500 in today's dollars. As of 2018, the median home in Cleveland was worth $71,100. (Homes that exist in Cleveland today are not necessarily the same houses that existed in 1980, so we can't directly apply the comparison to the change in value for a particular home.) By comparison, in 1980 the median home in the city of San Francisco was worth $330,580 (in today's dollars). In 2018, the median home in San Francisco was valued at $1,195,700.[8] Try this one easy trick to becoming a millionaire: buy a home in the right place at the right time, and stay put for thirty years! What could go wrong?

Even within the same city, when people buy and sell homes influences the returns on their investment. Homeowners and investors who were lucky enough to buy a house in the early 2000s and sell before 2007 realized unusually large returns. Those who bought near the market peak in 2006 were less fortunate: many homeowners lost all of their initial equity within a few years, and in some markets, prices have still not recovered. Metro areas like Las Vegas saw particularly volatile house price cycles, creating both big winners and big losers through housing wealth (figure 5-2).

Another drawback to storing all your savings in your home is that extracting cash from real estate is more complicated than fishing change out of a piggybank. In financial terms, housing is an illiquid asset: selling

FIGURE 5-2. Las Vegas housing prices are more volatile than the United States.

House price changes, 1991–2019.

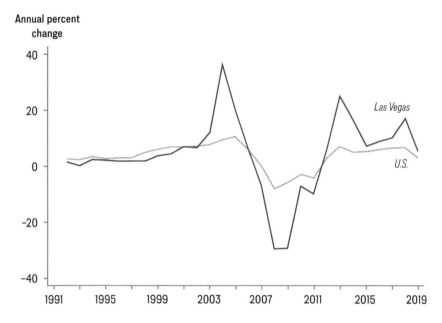

Annual percent change

Source: Federal Housing Finance Administration house price index, seasonally adjusted.

your house is a lengthy and complex process even under good market conditions. Financial assets like stocks and bonds can be sold for cash almost instantaneously, even during a recession. Listing a home for sale, finding a willing buyer, then waiting for the buyer to line up financing usually takes at least 30 to 60 days even in the hottest real estate market.[9] And while it is just as easy to convert $500 worth of stocks into cash as it is $20,000, you can't sell only part of your home. Homeowners can use tools such as home equity loans or cash-out refinancing to borrow against the equity they have accumulated, but access to these tools depends on having a strong credit rating and can increase the risk of default.[10] Importantly, homeowners with weaker income, assets, and credit will have the hardest time accessing the equity in their homes, especially during economic downturns.

Homeownership is at the root of the racial wealth gap

From a larger social perspective, the most important limitation of relying on homeownership for wealth-building is the persistent gap this has created in wealth held by Black and white families. Scholars have documented the long history of explicit racial discrimination codified by policies adopted and enforced by U.S. government agencies. In the nineteenth and early twentieth centuries, the deeds to many homes included racially restrictive covenants, clauses that prohibited sale of the property to Blacks, Jews, and other specified ethnic groups.[11] Even after enforcement of these restrictive covenants was struck down by a 1948 Supreme Court case, Black families continued to face legal barriers to buying homes.[12] White home buyers after World War II took advantage of federally backed (and implicitly subsidized) mortgage loans to purchase moderately priced new homes in the growing suburbs. But very few Black families were approved for Federal Housing Administration (FHA) loans. The FHA further used a practice known as redlining to prohibit mortgages being issued to white borrowers if they wanted to buy in a mostly Black neighborhood. Landlords could legally refuse to rent apartments to Black households because of their race; most U.S. cities developed stark racial dividing lines that separated Black and white neighborhoods, reinforced by racially motivated zoning, urban renewal programs, and development of the federal highway system.[13]

Explicit racial discrimination in housing was outlawed by the 1968 federal Fair Housing Act. Three activities within housing markets are particularly important in creating and reinforcing racially disparate outcomes—yet difficult for policymakers to monitor consistently for discrimination. Landlords decide which prospective tenants to rent their properties to. Real estate agents choose which homes and neighborhoods they show to prospective home buyers. And financial service companies underwrite applications for home purchase loans, determining which households receive mortgage loans and on what terms. The Fair Housing Act prohibited landlords, Realtors, and banks from

explicitly using race as a criterion in these decisions. In 1977, the federal
Community Reinvestment Act (CRA) was passed to strengthen oversight
of mortgage lending and reduce barriers for Black communities' access
to both mortgage loans and small business loans.[14]

But a law is only as effective as its enforcement. More than 50 years
after the Fair Housing Act, evidence of housing discrimination can still
be found in mortgage lending[15] and steering behavior by Realtors.[16]
Paired audit studies show continued differences in landlords' willing-
ness to rent to Black tenants, especially single mothers with children.
Native American households are less likely to obtain mortgages from
mainstream lenders.[17] Monitoring behavior and ensuring compliance
among the hundreds of thousands of individual real estate transactions
that occur in the United States every year would require substantially
more resources and political will than government agencies have shown
to date. The CRA is widely acknowledged to be in need of modernization
and strengthening, in order to reflect current banking realities.[18]

The barriers to homeownership faced by Black families (and to a
lesser degree, Latinos) have created a cumulative effect on wealth, or
rather the lack of wealth.[19] Families with wealth are able to pass along
advantages to the next generation; families with no wealth cannot.[20]
Young white adults looking to buy their first home often receive financial
assistance from parents or grandparents,[21] while young Black adults—
even those earning similar incomes—struggle to come up with cash for
a downpayment.[22] Within income tiers, Black households are substantially less likely than white households to own their home.

Black and Latino households who do purchase a home tend to build
less equity and are more vulnerable to default or foreclosure. Less wealth
translates into smaller downpayments, which means that Black and
Latino first-time home buyers are likely to buy lower-valued homes
and take on more debt as a share of purchase price, resulting in lower
levels of home equity.[23] As of 2015, 41 percent of black households and
45 percent of Latinos owned their home, compared to 71 percent of non-
Hispanic white households. The typical Black homeowner had about

$56,000 in home equity, while Latino homeowners had about $62,000 in equity, compared to $100,000 for non-Hispanic white homeowners, as shown in figure 5-3. The very high home equity numbers for Asian homeowners reflects greater concentration in high-cost housing markets, particularly on the West Coast.

In the leadup to the 2007–2009 foreclosure crisis, Black and Latino home buyers were more likely to have subprime loans, which come with higher interest rates and other terms that increase the probability of default.[24] The homeownership rate among Black households dropped from 46.6 percent in 2006 to 42 percent in 2019. While white and Asian homeownership rates have rebounded since the Great Recession, Black and Latino ownership has still not recovered. Wealth held by Black and Latino families has correspondingly declined during this period.[25]

FIGURE 5-3. Black and Latino homeowners have less home equity.
Median home equity (home value less outstanding mortgage balance) by race.

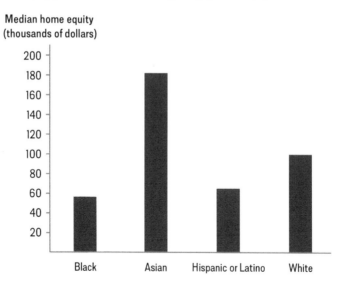

Source: U.S. Census Bureau, Survey of Income and Program Participation (2015).

Note: All groups are mutually exclusive (e.g., Black includes only non-Hispanic Blacks, Hispanic includes all races).

Advocates have called for a number of policy interventions to increase not only entry into homeownership by Black and Latino households but also more sustainable tenure.[26] While these interventions would help future home buyers build more equity, they would have no immediate impact on the racial wealth gap that has accumulated over 200 years.

Homevoters contribute to toxic politics

Overdependence on home equity leads to another unpleasant social consequence: homeowners react with hostility toward anything—or anyone—they believe will negatively impact their property values. Much of the economic rationale in favor of subsidizing homeownership rests on the assertion that homeowners create positive spillovers for society: they invest more in maintaining home quality, are more engaged with their children's education, show up more reliably to vote, and are generally more engaged in civic life.[27]

But homeowners' political engagement may not be unambiguously beneficial to society, if it primarily promotes their narrow financial interests at the expense of others—especially less affluent renters. William Fischel coined the term "homevoters" to describe how homeowners center much of their local political activity around protecting their own property values.[28] In practice, this often manifests itself as opposition to any changes in their community that they dislike, including those that would have broad social benefits, such as moderately priced housing.[29] As discussed in chapter 6, relying on property taxes to finance local services like schools compounds the problem. Community meetings tend to be dominated by older, white, male homeowners—even when most residents in the community are none of those things.[30] This pattern is largely independent of partisan affiliation. Homeowners in heavily Democratic suburbs throughout California, Massachusetts, and New York may clutch their pearls over former President Donald Trump's racist tweets, but when developers propose building low-income housing in their own communities, they vehemently oppose these perceived threats to their "Suburban Lifestyle Dream."[31]

In trying to discern the motives for wealthy homeowners' hostility toward affordable housing, it can be difficult to disentangle financial self-interest from racial or class animus. Households who rely almost exclusively on home equity for rainy-day savings or to finance their retirement will understandably worry about the value of their home declining. New housing development does create the need for more infrastructure, which must be paid for somehow (chapter 6). But these are practical concerns that could be addressed through better public policies. Expanding channels for wealth-building outside homeownership might not eliminate NIMBYism, but it could prompt some suburban homeowners to reflect on how much of their attachment to "preserving neighborhood character" is driven by animosity toward, or fear of, low-income households and people of color.

Solutions

To help households build more balanced and liquid savings portfolios, policymakers should pursue two approaches. First, they should redesign homeownership subsidies in the tax system to more precisely target moderate-income, first-time home buyers. Second, they should develop and incentivize wealth-building strategies that address the shortcomings of homeownership, including short-term liquidity and the racial wealth gap.

Redesign homeownership subsidies to be more effective and more equitable

Current policies that ostensibly encourage people to become homeowners are in fact poorly targeted at "marginal home buyers" and moreover are expensive and highly regressive. The largest and best-known subsidy is the mortgage interest deduction (MID). Households may subtract interest paid on mortgages for their primary or secondary homes from their federally taxable income. Prior to the 2017 Tax Cuts and Jobs

Act (TCJA), interest on mortgage balances up to $1 million was fully deductible; the TCJA lowered the threshold to $750,000.[32] The benefits of this subsidy flow overwhelmingly to high-income households, who are more likely to own their homes, own more expensive houses (thus have larger mortgage balances), and face higher marginal income tax rates.[33] The majority of homeowners now take the standard deduction, rather than itemizing, and so receive no benefit from the MID. According to the Urban-Brookings Tax Policy Center's calculations, nearly 80 percent of the benefits from the MID are claimed by households making over $152,000 (more than double the U.S. median income).[34]

Most people choose to buy their first home for reasons that have nothing to do with lowering their federal income tax liabilities. The transition from renting to owning generally accompanies major life events, like getting married, having a child, or reaching a higher-paying job.[35] There is little evidence to support the claim that the MID increases homeownership rates. Indeed, other wealthy countries that offer less preferential tax treatment for homeownership have homeownership rates similar to those in the United States.[36] Rather, the MID encourages people who would own their homes anyway to purchase more expensive homes and take on higher rates of leverage (larger mortgage balances relative to the purchase price)—not exactly socially desirable goals, for those seeking to justify the $30.2 billion annual cost of the program.[37]

A number of scholars have proposed ways that federal tax policy could more effectively enable moderate- and middle-income renters to purchase their first home. These differ somewhat in the details, but almost all share the general structure of targeting assistance at first-time buyers, rather than delivering annual subsidies to existing homeowners. One example proposed by Gale et al. (2007) involves two changes to current tax policies. First, convert the MID into a one-time refundable tax credit for first-time home buyers, with larger credits for lower-income households.[38] Second, to offset any disincentive this might create for renters to save for a downpayment, the federal government could create a new matched savings program, with preferential tax treatment as long as the savings are used to purchase a home or rolled into a qualified retirement account. These two prongs—helping households build a pot of savings to apply toward a downpayment, and offsetting the initial cost of purchasing a home through a refundable credit—would offer better support to moderate- and middle-income households, at substantially less public expense than the current subsidies.

Help all households build short-term liquidity through matched savings accounts

Both renters and homeowners would benefit from having some savings not tied to home equity. As the COVID-19 crisis has shown, a sudden economic shutdown can cause millions of workers to be unemployed for months at a time. Homeowners' financial obligations don't end once they move into their new house; being short of cash for unexpected maintenance and upkeep can threaten the stability of low- and moderate-income homeowners. In addition to redesigning homeownership subsidies, the federal government should develop and encourage mechanisms for short-term nonretirement savings.[39]

Almost everyone runs into unexpected yet urgent expenses from time to time. Air conditioners break in August, cars essential for the daily commute need new brake pads, dental work is not covered by health insurance. And yet, most U.S. households have little available cash to cover these situations. A frequently cited survey from the Federal Reserve estimates that 40 percent of households would need to borrow or sell assets to cover an unexpected $400 expense. Black and Latino households are less likely to have any liquid savings than non-Hispanic whites, and have substantially lower balances (figure 5-4). Behavioral economics offers some insights into why humans systematically don't set aside enough rainy-day savings. We place more weight on our happiness today than our unhappiness tomorrow, have limited ability to foresee negative shocks in the future, and are overly optimistic about our financial prospects improving.

Understanding the reasons behind our collective tendency to over-

FIGURE 5-4. Black and Latino families have smaller emergency savings than white families.
Presence of liquid assets and conditional mean value of assets.

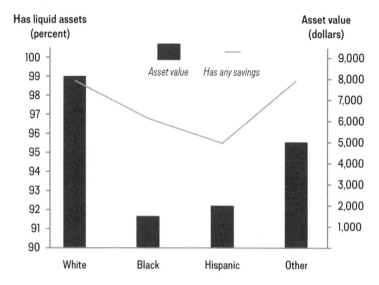

Source: Board of Governors of the Federal Reserve System, Survey of Consumer Finances (2019).

Note: Graph shows mean asset value for all households who have some savings (e.g., excludes households with zero asset balance).

spend today (or undersave for tomorrow), has led to several improvements in the design of retirement savings plans that could be applied to encourage rainy-day savings as well. Beshears et al. develop a proposal for an emergency savings plan that operates in many ways like 401(k) plans.[40] Workers would be automatically enrolled through their employer to have part of their paycheck deposited in a savings account set aside for unexpected preretirement needs. The automatic enrollment feature increases the likelihood that workers would participate. Setting up a separate account from both regular direct deposit (which workers spend on current needs, like rent and groceries) and retirement accounts (which generally impose a penalty for withdrawing funds before retirement age) helps households avoid tapping into their emergency savings for daily consumption. Such a program could also include matches from employers and could be eligible for preferred tax treatment, to further encourage workers to participate. A program of this structure could help both renter and homeowner households accumulate the type of easily accessible emergency savings that most households lack, without requiring substantial government subsidy.[41]

Address the racial wealth gap through individual and child development accounts

Families that have wealth tend to pass it along to subsequent generations: parents and grandparents help pay for children's college and chip in toward a first home purchase. These behaviors contribute to the persistence of racial wealth gaps. The typical white family with a household head under age thirty-five has net wealth around $24,000, whereas young Black families have only $600 in net wealth—less than a month's rent.[42] Young Latino families fall in between, with about $11,000 in wealth. To create a somewhat more equal playing field for people of all races whose families have little wealth will require some kind of circuit breaker: an up-front transfer of resources that provides everyone with seed money.

During the 2020 Democratic Presidential campaign, Senator Cory Booker called for the creation of child development accounts, sometimes referred to as "baby bonds."[43] His proposal draws on the work of economists Darrick Hamilton and W. S. Darrity, who recommend that the federal government issue grants to the families of newborn children, with the amount determined on a sliding scale based on the family's wealth.[44] Targeting the grants based on wealth instead of income has two advantages. First, current income can be a misleading indicator of a family's true resources, especially for young workers at the beginning of their career. That is, a young family earning $30,000 through part-time work and student stipends while enrolled in law school has much higher expected life-time earnings than a young family with only high school degrees working full-time minimum-wage jobs. Second, although such a program would be prima facie race neutral, because wealth disparities in the United States are even larger than income disparities, child development accounts would directly address the racial wealth gap. Some 85 percent of Black families have net worth below the median white family's wealth.[45] Depending on the specific design, Hamilton and Darrity estimate that three-quarters of newborn children could receive some funding through a child development account, with an average value of $20,000 and a maximum of $60,000. Funds could be accessed once the child reaches age eighteen for certain qualified uses, including education, starting a business, or the down payment on a home.

A similar concept, known as individual development accounts (IDAs), could encourage saving for medium- to long-term goals. For low-income households, their contributions could be matched by a federal subsidy. Accumulated savings can be accessed without penalty for certain purposes, including home purchase or repair, postsecondary education, or starting a business. To date IDAs have been established in the United States only as short-term pilot programs serving a limited number of households, although some scholars have proposed a universal version.[46] Evaluation of the pilot programs found that IDAs can increase access to homeownership and nonretirement financial asset holding among renters.[47]

Conclusion

The United States has historically relied heavily on homeownership as a strategy for household wealth-building. This offers some useful features, notably a forced savings mechanism and hedging against rents rising faster than income. There are also limitations from both individual and social perspectives. Housing is undiversified and illiquid, thus risky to households. Blacks and Latinos have largely been excluded from homeownership, due to decades of racial discrimination in housing and mortgage markets. Excess reliance on home equity also induces homeowners to fight against needed investments, such as affordable housing, that would have widespread social benefits—a problem that is further discussed in chapters 6 and 7. A more balanced set of federal tax policies could support first-time home buyers—including Black and Latino families who have traditionally been excluded from homeownership— while supporting both renters and owners to develop savings through alternative vehicles.

6

High-Quality Community Infrastructure Is Expensive, But It Benefits Everyone

Attend any community meeting where a proposal for a new housing development is on the agenda, and existing residents will raise two main objections: schools and parking. More housing will bring additional children, putting stress on existing school buildings, teachers, and counselors. And more homes translate into more cars, increasing traffic congestion and taking up more (publicly owned, usually underpriced) on-street parking. Sometimes opponents of housing growth use these excuses in bad faith to cover for other concerns, like racial or economic bias, but the concerns are not entirely unfounded. A community that is growing in population and housing will increase demand for local infrastructure, which must be paid for somehow.

The relationship between housing and public services is more complicated than it sometimes appears at public meetings. Population growth and decline, as well as demographic changes, all impact the demand for infrastructure. There isn't one simple answer to the question of who should pay for infrastructure. How infrastructure is financed and provided has important implications for economic and racial equity:

some funding mechanisms lead to larger differences in the quality of infrastructure enjoyed by poor and wealthy communities.

In the United States, we usually think of local governments as the primary providers of services like schools and roads. In practice, local, regional, state, and federal agencies help pay for a wide range of infrastructure. The private sector—businesses and developers—also own, pay for, or provide infrastructure, through general taxes and dedicated finance mechanisms like impact fees. Who pays, and through what channel, varies widely across states, because state governments write the rules under which local governments are allowed to raise revenue. Time is also an important dimension of "who pays." Many infrastructure projects create long-lived capital that benefits generations of future taxpayers, as well as current residents, so the costs can be shared over time. Elected officials also find it politically appealing to defer fiscal responsibility onto future generations, or otherwise shift costs away from current taxpayers.

Community infrastructure is a lot more than roads and bridges

The term "infrastructure" gets thrown around a lot without specifying exactly what it means. When used in built environment conversations, infrastructure typically means the physical systems that support cities and towns: roads, bridges, public transit, water and sewer systems, and broadband internet service. Going farther upstream, infrastructure includes the network of energy producers and distributors (power plants and grid operators that produce and disseminate electricity).

Alternatively, we can define infrastructure more broadly to include the economic and social institutions that support communities: schools and child care; libraries, parks, and recreation facilities; hospitals, clinics, and other health care providers. Neighborhood-serving retail and services, such as grocery stores, pharmacies, laundromats, banks, and coffeeshops enable people and businesses to carry out their daily activities. Even subsidized housing can be considered economic infrastructure because it enables lower-wage workers to live near their jobs.

The COVID-19 pandemic cast new light on why place-based economic and social institutions are critical to communities. Access to high-quality child care and schools enables parents to participate in the labor force, besides doing the important work of educating future workers and citizens. Twenty-first-century libraries do much more than loan out books: they offer reliable, publicly available internet access, assistance with job searches, and learning resources for students of all ages. Public parks and private "third places" like coffeeshops and restaurants provide spaces for social and professional person-to-person interactions, from job interviews and networking events to family birthday parties.[1] During the pandemic, employees at grocery stores and pharmacies were designated "essential workers," in the same category as utility workers and bus drivers. Communities cannot function well without these institutions.

High-quality community infrastructure benefits all current residents and will attract more people to move to the locality, driving future economic growth. As discussed in chapter 2, the quality of local public schools is an important component of housing values: people will pay more for homes in the catchment zones for highly desirable schools than otherwise identical homes elsewhere. This has important implications for financing: the quality of infrastructure is capitalized into property values, which then feeds back into local revenues collected through property taxes, which in turn can be used to maintain and upgrade infrastructure.[2] Even the expectation of future infrastructure improvements can cause property values to rise.[3] The feedback cycle works in reverse too: poor communities with limited resources to invest in local infrastructure tend to suffer from declining property values and declining revenues, which can lead to lower-quality services.

Some types of infrastructure we think of as being a public responsibility—roads and schools—while others—grocery stores and laundromats—are provided by the private sector, although in reality the lines between public and private are often blurry. One important distinction is whether a particular type of infrastructure can be sustainably financed through charging access for use.[4] Grocery stores cover their operating costs by charging shoppers money for the goods they consume, while people who can't afford groceries aren't allowed to take them. By contrast, public schools must provide spaces for all children, regardless of families' ability to pay. As we shall see, many forms of infrastructure fall somewhere between completely private financing and completely public financing.

Expanding infrastructure for a growing population costs money

When a community grows in population and housing, it leads to an increased demand for physical, economic, and social infrastructure. But the relationship between growth and infrastructure needs can be complicated; for instance, an increase in the population of older adults will have a greater impact on health care systems than on primary and secondary schools. The type of housing that gets built, and where housing is added, also matters.

When forecasting the infrastructure needs generated by new housing, it is useful to distinguish between two different types of development that vary in their physical and financial impacts on communities. "Greenfields" development occurs when previously undeveloped open space is converted into housing or commercial space; for instance, farmland on the outskirts of a large metro becomes a new suburban subdivision. Infill development refers to replacing existing structures with newly built ones, usually at a higher density; for example, redeveloping a single-story shopping center surrounded by surface parking into midrise apartments.[5] Greenfields sites by definition lack the physical infrastructure needed to support housing. The developer, local government, or both must build roads and sidewalks connecting the new homes to existing neighborhoods, as well as extending connections to water and sewer systems (or equipping the homes with wells and septic systems). Infill developments can often make use of existing physical infrastructure, although systems may need upgrading or "rightsizing" for the new project.[6]

Beyond the minimum necessity of roads, water, sewer, and utilities, greenfield and infill development have different implications for economic and social infrastructure, in part because they typically include different types of homes. Most new homes built in suburban greenfield sites are single-family, detached homes or townhomes. Infill developments are more likely to be attached homes or multifamily buildings, especially in expensive locations in the urban core. Structure type is a good predictor of home size. In new apartment buildings, more than 80 percent of units are studio, one- and two-bedroom units. Among newly built single-family homes, over 40 percent have three or more bedrooms.[7] One specific type of infill development that does not change the number of homes—but can lead to higher housing prices—is teardown and replacement of existing small single-family homes with newer, larger single-family homes.[8]

Differences in home size are strongly correlated with characteristics of residents who move into new housing—which means different impacts on public services. Large homes are more likely to attract families with school-age children, whereas smaller homes tend to be chosen by people living alone or couples without children. On average, a new subdivision with 200 single-family houses will generate more demand for local schools than a 200-unit apartment building. Schools are one of the more expensive infrastructure components, which figures largely into public debates over housing growth. The fiscal impact on schools is not simply a matter of the number of children added; age, family income, and parents' education also influence per-pupil costs, as well as the potential for school aid provided by state and federal governments. (Everything related to school financing is complicated, as we'll see throughout the chapter.) Home size and type also have an impact on environmental demands: larger homes have a bigger carbon footprint, requiring more energy for heating and cooling. Apartments use less water than detached homes; they have fewer bathrooms and no lawns to keep hydrated.

The demands on infrastructure for each additional home—the marginal infrastructure cost—isn't a smooth linear function. Schools again offer a clear example. A new housing development that adds a handful of additional kids to the nearest school, say three or four per grade level, can probably be accommodated by existing teachers, counselors, classrooms, and equipment. That is, the per-child cost of a few more students may be relatively small. But if each teacher is expected to teach no more than twenty-five students, then adding the twenty-sixth student might require hiring a teacher's aide—a large increase in costs associated with one extra student. The same logic applies to most types of infrastructure. Adding one more rider to a half-full bus costs almost nothing, but once that bus is at maximum capacity, buying a second bus and hiring another driver are expensive. This lumpiness of infrastructure funding—marginal costs increase at irregular intervals—can make it difficult for local governments to plan for and finance appropriate investments, especially when trying to set the "correct" price for a new housing development.

Maintaining existing infrastructure costs money too

In 1950, the city of St. Louis had over 850,000 residents. By 2019, the population was just over 300,000. Much of the city's physical infrastructure was built to support its peak population, so the city is essentially overbuilt relative to its needs today—a common problem among older industrial cities in the Northeast and Midwest. Because roads and water pipes last a very long time, St. Louis still has to pay for operations and maintenance of its legacy infrastructure systems, but there are fewer residents and businesses left to contribute.

What can cities do when faced with this situation? One option is to cut back on the quantity or quality of services. Another is to raise fees on remaining residents. Think about how this works with schools. For small population drops, the number of kids per class falls. At some point, principals have to consolidate multiple classes, which means they don't need as many teachers. Eventually, the district may decide to shutter entire schools—causing kids who still live in the neighborhood to transfer to other schools, farther from where they live.[9]

Once population decline has led to reduced quality of public services, it risks becoming a downward spiral. Residents with more resources are often the first households to move, leaving behind fewer—and poorer—families. Breaking this cycle may require financial intervention from state or federal agencies, which have more resources and greater fiscal flexibility than local governments. Anchor institutions, such as universities, hospitals, and large employers that choose to stay in the community, can help slow population and economic decline but cannot by themselves fill the gap left by shrinking public resources.

Even cities with a stable population size have to plan for periodic reinvestments in their infrastructure to avoid declining service quality. Just as individual property owners need to replace worn-out roofs or heating systems from time to time, cities have to upgrade pipes, roads, bus systems, and public buildings. Climate change is putting additional stresses on a wide range of local infrastructure. Extreme rainfall exceeds the capacity of storm sewers, which then overflow, causing toxic materials to flow in the streets or back up into homes.[10] Rising temperatures and prolonged periods of excess heat mean increased demand for air-conditioning; communities from California to Texas are becoming all too familiar with the disruptions to daily life and safety hazards when electricity providers cannot meet spikes in demand.[11]

Local governments rely heavily on property taxes to pay for community infrastructure

Local governments can raise money in a variety of ways to pay for community infrastructure. We can group them into three broad categories: direct taxes and fees, indirect taxes, and debt financing (table 6-1).

Each type of fiscal tool has distinct advantages and disadvantages, raising questions about economic efficiency, political attractiveness, equity, and legal feasibility. In practice, most local governments rely on a bundle of multiple fiscal tools to pay for locally provided goods and services. Some state governments have chosen to prohibit local governments from using certain tools (known as pre-emption). And the "optimal" set of taxes—which goods and services to tax, and at what rates—varies depending on the economic characteristics of each local community.

Some key tradeoffs include the following: How broadly should costs be spread across people and businesses in the community? Should the full costs of investments be paid up front, or distributed over current and future spending? What are the equity implications (e.g., how are low-income people or places affected)?

User fees, or direct charges per good or service consumed, are the closest public sector equivalent to how private sector companies finance their activities. Bus fares, toll roads, and water and sewer fees billed to property owners are all examples of user fees charged by local governments. An economic advantage to user fees is that they encourage people to consider the value of the good or service they consume, relative to the cost they pay. Toll roads that have variable fees based on traffic congestion show how user fees can benefit the larger community. Drivers who choose to drive on main roads during peak commuting times—when every additional car causes more inconvenience to all drivers—face higher out-of-pocket tolls than drivers who shift their commute to times when roads are less crowded. When set appropriately, user fees can help conserve scarce resources, like discouraging property owners from watering their lawn during droughts.

Not all publicly provided goods and services are well suited to financing through user fees. Bus fares and road tolls can be set to cover the marginal cost of those services—the cost of one additional passenger or driver. But it is not practical to rely on user fees for large-scale investments, like building dedicated bus lanes or resurfacing highways. And there are serious equity concerns (not to mention legal issues) about

TABLE 6-1. Financial tools available to pay for community infrastructure.

CATEGORY	EXAMPLE	DIRECT PAYER(S)	INDIRECT PAYER(S)
Direct taxes and fees	User fees	People and companies that use services (e.g., water, transit)	
	Property taxes	Residential and commercial property owners	Renters (people and businesses)
	Sales taxes	Buyers of taxable goods and services	Sellers of taxable goods and services
	Income taxes (personal)	Residents with taxable income	
	Wage taxes	Local businesses and workers	
Indirect taxes	Exactions and impact fees	Developers of new housing/commercial property	Buyers/renters of new housing; landowners
	Inclusionary zoning	Developers of new housing	Buyers/renters of new market-rate housing
	Fiscal zoning	Buyers or renters of new housing	
Debt financing	Municipal bonds	Current and future residents	

Note: The list of indirect payers is not comprehensive. Determining the full economic incidence of fiscal tools is complicated and depends on design and implementation of specific policies.

charging user fees for essential services, such as requiring poor families to pay the marginal cost of their children's attendance at public schools. For goods where user fees are strongly preferred to discourage overuse, pairing them with subsidies that cover a minimum level of service for lower-income households can mitigate equity concerns.

Property taxes are the bread-and-butter of local government revenues (figure 6-1). Nearly every city and county levies taxes based on the value of real estate, covering both homes and nonresidential properties.[12] Nationally, nearly half of local government revenues (excluding state and federal aid) come from property taxes.[13] Property taxes are charged as a percent of assessed values, often with exemptions for some portion of the home's value (e.g., the first $50,000). The average statutory property tax rate is slightly over 1 percent, but rates vary considerably across states and localities.

FIGURE 6-1. Local governments rely heavily on property taxes.
Percent of own-source local government revenue, 2017.

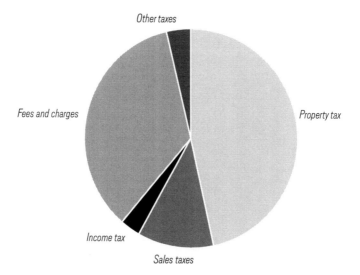

Source: Urban-Brookings Tax Policy Center, *Briefing Book: The State of State (and Local) Tax Policy* (2021). Excludes transfers from state and federal governments (www.taxpolicycenter.org/briefing-book/what-are-sources-revenue -local-governments).

Determining whether property taxes are progressive—meaning that they fall more heavily on higher-income households—is quite tricky.[14] In one sense, property taxes function like a wealth tax, applied against a major financial asset.[15] How much home buyers are willing to spend on a home often reflects expectations of future income, rather than current annual income. People who anticipate having higher long-term wealth (say, a young couple with professional degrees from prestigious schools) tend to buy more expensive homes than people with similar current income but lower future expectations. In this sense, property taxes are generally progressive. Property taxes can also be viewed as a tax on housing consumption: although renters do not explicitly pay property taxes, some portion of the landlord's bill is implicitly built into their rent. Viewed as a consumption tax, property taxes can be regressive. In practice, how the burden of property taxes falls on households of different income, wealth, and race depends in large part on how local governments design and implement property taxes—including the accuracy and consistency of assessing underlying property values.[16]

Compared to user fees, property taxes are a broad-based form of revenue: the amount each household or company contributes toward locally provided infrastructure and services does not depend on how much they use any particular service. Taxes collected from households with and without school-aged children all contribute to the support of public schools. Households that primarily ride public transit pay taxes that support road maintenance. As discussed in chapter 7, the fact that property tax revenues (and other forms of general revenue) are used to pay for a wide range of locally provided services and infrastructure creates incentives for households to sort themselves into localities with economically and demographically similar residents.

Local governments can structure their property taxes in slightly different ways, either for political advantage or to achieve other social goals. One notable option is that they can set different tax rates for residential and commercial properties, thereby lowering the statutory burden on current residents (voters). Communities that have large busi-

ness districts—both cities with traditional downtown centers and suburbs that are home to large shopping centers or office parks—often set a
higher millage rate on commercial properties than residential ones. One
popular feature is a homestead exemption, under which owners who live
in their homes pay taxes on less than 100 percent of the assessed value.
For instance, the District of Columbia deducts approximately $76,000
from homeowners' assessed value subject to taxes.[17] The economic rationale most frequently offered for homestead exemptions is to reduce the
tax burden on lower-income homeowners, for whom the exempt amount
is a larger share of overall home value. It also reflects a larger policy bias
that homeowners are somehow "better" citizens (which is not unambiguously true, as discussed in chapter 5). Many localities have special
exemptions or waivers for older adults whose homes have appreciated
substantially over time, but who are retired and have limited current
income. Certain categories of property owners, including government
agencies, churches, and universities, are often exempted from standard
property taxes and instead negotiate arrangements for payments in lieu
of taxes (known as PILOTs).

These variations in what kinds of properties are subject to taxes,
and how much they pay, can add up to big impacts on the total amount
of revenues that local governments are able to collect. And they affect
the incentives for local governments to allow—or prohibit—new development of various types. Localities that are permitted to charge higher
taxes on commercial properties may be more inclined to approve con-
version of vacant land for retail or office projects (which don't directly
increase demand for schools or social services) rather than for housing.

State governments create the rules that guide local governments'
taxing and spending authority (restrictions on these powers are known
as tax expenditure limits, or TELs). As of 2018, forty-four states and the
District of Columbia had established some limits on property taxation.[18]
Some directly cap the maximum tax rate that can be levied. Others limit
the amount by which taxes can increase each year, either by restricting
the increase in assessed value or the total amount of taxes charged.

The most famous (or notorious) example of this is California's Proposition 13. Adopted in 1978, it sets a maximum property tax rate of 1 percent, and allows the assessed value to rise no more than 2 percent each year in between sales—regardless of how much the market value of the home increases.[19] The California Legislative Analyst's Office, which analyzes the state's fiscal condition, has estimated how much tax relief Prop 13 provides to long-term homeowners—and conversely, the cost of Prop 13 to local governments in lost revenues.[20]

To understand how much Prop 13 distorts property tax revenues, consider a simple example from the Legislative Analyst's Office report. In 1980, a typical house in California sold for around $100,000. Under the 2 percent assessed value cap, by 2015 that house would be valued at around $200,000 for property tax purposes—but the market value would have been nearly $500,000. Thus a homeowner who bought a typical home in 1980 and continued to own it in 2015 would be paying $2,000 per year in taxes on a half-million-dollar home. Someone who purchased an identical home in 2015—the same size and condition, located immediately adjacent—would owe $5,000 in property taxes.

Prop 13 has produced windfall gains—minimal taxation on assets with extraordinary rates of appreciation—for long-term California homeowners, especially those in coastal metros where housing values have risen the most. Until 2020, reduced property tax assessments could even be passed on from long-term homeowners to their children—an unusual and highly valuable intergenerational wealth transfer. By contrast, newcomers to California and first-generation home buyers pay property taxes on the full market value of their homes. Reflecting demographic changes in the state, Prop 13's benefits overwhelmingly accrue to higher-income white households.[21]

Over time, California's cities and counties have come to rely more heavily on other types of taxes, including local sales tax, utility tax, and hotel tax, as well as impact fees on new development. As discussed later in this chapter, sales taxes hit harder on lower-income households, while impact fees raise the cost of entry to communities.

Although California's state restrictions on property taxes are the best known, nearly half of all states place some limits around local governments' authority on property taxes.[22] In states where local governments have been severely limited in their ability to raise general taxes, cities and counties rely more heavily on indirect taxes to fund community infrastructure: mechanisms like impact fees and fiscal zoning, discussed later in the chapter. These tools potentially create much larger distortions in housing markets and are particularly unfriendly toward lower-cost housing. More generally, binding constraints on local taxing authority can hinder local governments' ability to handle unexpected fiscal situations, such as the sharp drop in property values causes by the Great Recession and plummeting sales tax revenues during the COVID-19 pandemic.[23]

Relying on property taxes to fund local services leads to widely varying quality across jurisdictions: cities and counties with high poverty rates tend to have low property values, making it hard to maintain and invest in public services. As discussed in the solutions section later in the chapter, this can be mitigated with more revenue sharing across jurisdictions, such as state and federal aid.

In thirty-eight states, local governments are permitted to levy sales taxes, in addition to those assessed by state governments.[24] Local sales tax rates range from less than 0.5 percent to more than 5 percent in states where they are permitted. As with property taxes, state governments can set upper limits on sales tax rates, as well as define what goods and services can be taxed. Many states exempt groceries from sales taxes or tax them at a lower rate than nonfood items.[25] By contrast, food bought at restaurants is taxed. Tobacco, alcohol, and gasoline are often taxed at a higher rate to discourage consumption (sometimes referred to as "sin taxes"). For cities and counties where out-of-jurisdiction commuters or tourists constitute a substantial portion of shoppers, sales taxes offer local governments a way to raise revenues from nonresidents. Sales taxes are one of the more transparent forms of taxation, because shoppers see the taxes printed on their bills when they buy goods and services. Sales taxes are more regressive than either property or income taxes because poor people spend a larger share of their income on essential goods and services.

Income taxes are the least frequently used form of general taxation by local governments; about 3,800 municipalities and 190 counties have some local income tax. Prevalence varies widely across states, with Indiana, Maryland, and Pennsylvania having higher frequency.[26] New York City is one of the few large cities with a local income tax. Some cities, such as Philadelphia, have local wage taxes, which must be paid by anyone who works within the city boundaries, regardless of where they live.[27] In general, localities are wary of imposing income taxes, unless other cities and counties in the region have them as well, because it is relatively easy for tax-averse residents to avoid these by moving to neighboring jurisdictions. Wage taxes are harder for individual workers to avoid, although high wage taxes can encourage employers to relocate to lower-tax jurisdictions.

To pay for large investments, local governments have shifted from borrowing to indirect taxes

Infrastructure finance is challenging for local governments because costs are uneven over time. Developing new infrastructure requires big up-front investments, followed by more stable and predictable annual maintenance and operations, and periodic reinvestments for upgrades or expansions—cycles common to most capital projects. Although property taxes, sales taxes, and user fees may be enough to cover regular maintenance and operations, they are not a practical way to finance large investments for development or upgrades.

During the course of the twentieth century, local governments made a fundamental shift in how they pay for lump-sum infrastructure investments.[28] From the 1890s through the 1920s—a period notable for large-scale urbanization and modern infrastructure-building in the United States—local governments financed extensions to water and

sewer systems and other utilities through a combination of general revenues, long-term debt, and special assessments. (Some of the early mass
transit systems, including electric streetcars, were financed by private
companies rather than the public sector.)[29]

Cities and counties issued municipal bonds to raise capital from
private investors for large infrastructure projects, then the bonds would
be paid off over time (often decades) using general tax revenues. Using
long-term debt is an economically efficient solution for projects with
a long lifespan because it spreads the costs of projects over multiple
generations of a city's residents, all of whom benefit from having high-
quality infrastructure.[30] Since the adoption of a federal income tax in
1913, interest payments on municipal bonds (issued by both state and
local governments) have been exempted from federal income tax. This
creates an implicit federal subsidy for locally financed infrastructure;
local governments are able to borrow money at lower interest rates than
private firms, at the cost of reduced federal tax revenues.

While local and state governments still use long-term debt to pay for
some infrastructure projects, since the 1920s (and especially post–World
War II) there has been increasing reliance on a new mechanism: exactions from private developers.[31] State laws authorized local governments
to require developers who were building subdivisions to provide land
on site for roads, sidewalks, schools, fire stations, and similar public
uses—essentially a donation of land to the local government. Over time,
this practice of exacting land for public use evolved to allow developers
to meet their obligation through off-site contributions of land, and later
through cash payments, known as impact fees.

The U.S. Supreme Court has ruled that local governments may charge
developers impact fees to cover part or all of the infrastructure costs
associated with development: the amount of the fees and how the pro-
ceeds are used should conform to a "rational nexus" between the proposed development and demands on public services.[32] That is, developers
building a new subdivision can be required to pay fees that offset hiring
an additional teacher and expanding playgrounds at the neighborhood

school that children in the new subdivision will attend, but the local government should not require one developer to pay for expanding school facilities throughout the entire city. The nexus concept also applies to nonresidential construction: developers who propose to construct new office buildings or retail space can be required to pay "linkage" fees for associated services, such as investments in public transit or space for child care facilities. Exactions can be applied to a wide range of services, including water, sewer, school construction, parks and open space, traffic mitigation, stormwater drainage, fire and police services, and affordable housing. Inclusionary zoning programs are a popular variation on impact fees, in which developers are required to set aside homes for low-income households as part of market-rate housing developments.[33]

The prevalence of exactions to pay for infrastructure increased rapidly during the post–World War II period. Before 1960, exactions were quite rare, but by the mid-1980s, 90 percent of local governments used some form of exactions.[34] In theory, impact fees offer a tidy solution to the problem faced by growing communities, by making developers—and the consumers of newly built homes—take into account the costs they impose on existing residents.[35] Shifting costs away from current residents is politically popular, making impact fees attractive to local elected officials. In practice, impact fees raise several concerns. How accurately do local governments set the level of impact fees, relative to the true costs imposed by new housing? Who ultimately bears the cost of impact fees? Are impact fees better or worse than other financing mechanisms, from an equity perspective?

Predicting how additional housing will impact the demand for locally provided goods and services is complicated. As discussed earlier in the chapter, use of public services depends on the size and characteristics of the home and its inhabitants, only some of which are observable to the local government in advance. A subdivision of large, detached homes will likely attract families with school-age children, but also some households who do not use public schools. Households that own multiple cars and commute long distances put more demands on roads than transit commuters or retirees. Some local governments have a schedule of impact fees that vary by home size and location (generally higher for greenfields development than infill), which tries to account for these differences.[36] More often, impact fees are determined on a project-by-project basis through negotiation between developers and local governments. (Separate negotiations between a developer and multiple agencies within the same city or county are not unusual.) This can lead to wide variation in the effective fee charged per home, with little economic rationale behind the differences.[37] There are risks to setting impact fees either too high or too low, relative to the true demand for public services. Excessively high fees make housing too expensive for many consumers and are likely to discourage some projects from being built. If the fees are too low, then new homes become a fiscal drag on the local government. The negotiation process between developers and local governments further adds to the length, complexity, and costs of development—all of which translates into more expensive finished housing.

Who ultimately bears the cost of impact fees can vary over time and geography. One possibility is that the developer passes along the full amount of the impact fees to customers who buy or rent the finished housing. A second possibility is that the developer, anticipating the additional costs imposed by the impact fees, negotiates a lower price when buying the land, so previous landowners bear the costs. Third, if the developer has already purchased the land and consumers are not willing to pay higher costs for new housing once the project is finished, the impact fees will come out of the developer's profit. Often the reality lies somewhere between these scenarios, with costs being split between consumers, landowners, and the developer.

Underlying housing market conditions influence how costs are shared between these parties. In markets with very strong demand and limited supply—such as large coastal metros with highly restrictive zoning—developers are better able to pass along costs to consumers. Developers' choice sets are shaped by how prevalent impact fees are within a metro area. In regions like California where impact fees are widespread, developers cannot easily avoid fees by choosing to build projects in a neighboring city or county. In regions where impact fees are less common, or where there is substantial variation in the level of impact fees, cities and towns that set high fees are likely to see less new housing development—which may suit the existing residents just fine.

Impact fees raise some equity concerns. Because impact fees are effectively a tax on new homes, they are likely to reduce the amount of new development, relative to what would have been built otherwise. Like excessively restrictive zoning described in chapter 2, high impact fees limit the overall supply of homes in a region while driving up rents and prices—which is particularly harmful to low-income families. Over time, communities with high impact fees will see a change in resident characteristics. New housing is generally more expensive than older homes of similar size in the same community; impact fees make this difference more pronounced. The people who can afford to buy or rent expensive new homes are likely to have higher incomes than the community's existing residents—gentrification by impact fees.

Indeed, an alternative way of shifting responsibility for local public services onto new, higher-income residents can be achieved without impact fees, through an approach known as "fiscal zoning."[38] For any given property tax rate, a local government can raise more total revenues from more expensive homes: 1 percent of a $500,000 home yields $5,000 in annual property taxes, while 1 percent of a $200,000 home yields $2,000. If newly built homes are more expensive than existing homes, then average property tax revenues collected per home will increase, allowing the community to spend more money on public services without raising tax rates on existing residents. Zoning rules that require very large minimum lot sizes for new homes are an effective tool of fiscal zoning, and thus are attractive to homeowners even if they are not personally opposed to having low-income families as neighbors. That fiscally motivated zoning and zoning intended to maintain racial and economic segregation look virtually identical in practice can make

it difficult for researchers and policymakers to discern underlying motives—a problem for using fair housing laws to challenge racial discrimination. And the effects of fiscal zoning on housing outcomes—larger
homes on large lots, higher housing prices—exacerbate low-density
development patterns and long commutes, which fall disproportionately
on lower-income workers.

Solutions

A more economically efficient, environmentally sustainable, and
equitable approach to infrastructure finance should meet four goals:
encourage housing development that makes better use of existing infrastructure, mitigate income and racial disparities in access to high-
quality public services, reduce local governments' financial incentives to
oppose new housing, and accurately reflect social and economic costs of
new development at the regional rather than the local scale.

Encourage housing development that makes better use of existing infrastructure

Building new infrastructure is expensive and environmentally damaging. The cost of building roads, trains, and other systems have risen
sharply since the 1970s, so the marginal cost of adding homes that require new infrastructure is much higher than reusing and upgrading
existing capital.[39] Most U.S. metro areas have excess capacity in existing
systems. Older industrial cities in the Northeast and Midwest built their
roads, water, and sewer systems to serve much larger populations than
currently live there, yet continue to add housing through greenfields
suburban development. The central cities in newer Sunbelt metros like
Atlanta and Houston were built at much lower initial densities and offer
substantial opportunities for infill development: Los Angeles has built
thousands of new housing units in its downtown core by redeveloping
surface parking lots. Even in high-cost metros with vibrant urban cores,
there is ample room to add housing in centrally located neighborhoods.

The New York City, Boston, and San Francisco metros all have numerous subway or commuter rail stations surrounded by older, low-rise buildings—an inefficient use of both infrastructure and valuable land.

Some of the tools that would encourage more environmentally friendly housing development, such as taxes on driving and building energy usage, would also encourage more efficient use of infrastructure in the urban core. As discussed in chapter 3, making it more expensive for households to live in low-density, car-dependent outer suburbs would channel more development into infill locations. In metros with regulatory barriers that limit higher-density housing in expensive neighborhoods in the urban core, as discussed in chapter 2, zoning reforms are critical to enable infill development that the market already wants to provide.

Another tool that would help encourage infill development is to structure property taxes differently: charge higher rates on land than on structures.[40] Typically, the property tax rate set by local governments applies equally to land and any structures or "improvements" built on the land. Consider how this affects development incentives for parking lot owners in downtown Phoenix. If they decide to replace the parking lots with apartment buildings, the structure value of the properties increase considerably, resulting in a higher property tax bill. By contrast, if land is taxed at a higher rate than structures, then redeveloping parking lots or other low-density uses into apartments, offices, or retail would have less impact on the owner's property tax bill.[41]

Increasing tax rates on land would have the greatest impact on expensive land currently developed at low density. In the context of residential neighborhoods, areas that were originally developed as single-family homes with large yards and have seen rapid land value appreciation now offer opportunities for higher-density redevelopment. While relaxing zoning constraints on these neighborhoods would lead to gradual redevelopment, pairing zoning reforms with increased taxes on land values would encourage faster transitions. Moreover, a split-rate property tax would allow local governments to capture some of the increased value created by large-scale upzoning.[42] This approach offers particular appeal for places where the local government has invested in infrastructure, such as public transportation. Increasing taxes on land has also been tried as a strategy to combat vacancy and blight in cities that have seen substantial population loss.[43]

Mitigate racial and economic disparities in access to high-quality public services

Relying on local government revenues to fund community infrastructure will inevitably lead to gaps in service quality, regardless of how local governments raise revenues. Cities and counties with less affluent residents are disadvantaged in their capacity to pay for high-quality physical, social, and economic infrastructure. The quality of local public services is capitalized into housing prices, which further contributes to revenue gaps. Poor-quality services and lower home values in turn make it difficult to attract and retain higher-income households and businesses, putting further strain on the existing tax base.

While some locally provided services are funded primarily through local revenues, the United States does have an extensive system of redistribution through intergovernmental transfers (e.g., payments from one unit of government to another), some earmarked for locally provided services. The federal government provides grants to state and local governments for transportation, based on receipts of the federal gas tax. Roughly three-quarters of federal transportation spending is designated for roads, whereas less than one-quarter is directed to public transit and other noncar modes, such as bike lanes and sidewalk improvements—a system better designed for car-dependent suburbs than central cities.[44] The largest low-income housing subsidy program, housing vouchers, is funded by the federal government but administered through local agencies. The Community Development Block Grant Program, administered by the U.S. Department of Housing and Urban Development, allocates funds to states, large cities, and counties that can be used for a range of housing, economic, and community development purposes.[45] Federal funding is especially critical for programs targeted at low-income households or communities, because local governments with high concentrations of poverty have fewer resources to help their residents.

States also redistribute money across places to help mitigate differences in ability to pay for public services. Redistribution programs walk a delicate line: trying to provide enough funding to meaningfully improve service quality in low-income communities while not creating incentives for high-income communities to cut back their own spending. Most notably, over the past forty years, states have increasingly tried to lessen the differences in school spending between wealthy and poor districts.[46] The size of spending gaps varies widely across states, based on the extent of redistribution and the ways programs are designed. In general, school finance equalization programs provide more funding to school districts with a higher proportion of low-income students. (The federal government also provides some education funding aimed at helping poor children; federal funds constitute less than 10 percent of all K–12 spending.)[47]

Some statewide school finance equalization programs have been more effective than others at improving educational outcomes of low-income students, in part because of differences in how states have designed and implemented policies. Because the quality of local services is capitalized into property values, any policy that redistributes funds across localities for locally provided services (not just schools) must be carefully designed to avoid perverse incentives. For example, increased taxes on affluent cities and counties could cause them to cut local spending on schools, which could drive down property values in affluent communities, thereby limiting the total tax base available.[48] Programs that lead high-income households to send their children to private school, or to move across local jurisdictions to avoid higher taxes (an easier "escape" than moving across state boundaries) may also be counterproductive.

There are serious political hurdles to enacting statewide policies that improve housing outcomes, including redistribution. State legislatures are made up of representatives from the same cities and counties who often adopt narrowly self-interested policies. School finance equalization points toward another path for state action: state supreme courts ordered redistribution in California, Connecticut, New Jersey, and Ohio, among other states. Chapter 8 discusses some of the pros and cons of legislative action versus court intervention to achieve more equitable housing outcomes.

Reduce local governments' financial incentives to oppose new housing

Excessively high impact fees are a serious obstacle to housing production and affordability in states like California. But it is unrealistic to expect local governments to lower impact fees—or stop using fiscal zoning—as long as their hands are tied in using other, more efficient and equitable fiscal tools to pay for infrastructure.[49] Repealing or substantially reforming Prop 13 is therefore a necessary step in fixing California's perennial housing shortfall. Other states that have imposed binding limits on local governments' revenue authority should consider relaxing these rules as well.

During periods when interest rates are low (like now), local governments with strong credit ratings and manageable debt levels shouldn't be afraid to pay for long-term infrastructure with debt. Improved public transit infrastructure, replacing lead water pipes, and investments in the energy efficiency of schools and other public buildings will create economic, health, and environmental benefits for generations to come. Spreading the costs of these projects over current and future beneficiaries makes economic sense. Taking on more debt isn't feasible or advisable for all local governments; some localities already have high debt levels or poor credit ratings. The Great Recession may have made localities too debt shy, because the steep drop in local revenues forced them to choose between cutting current services and defaulting on debt payments. (Most local governments have balanced budget rules that hinder short-term flexibility.) But for the subset of local governments with healthy credit ratings and strong balance sheets, taking advantage of cheap capital for long-term investments would create fewer economic distortions or equity concerns than impact fees and fiscal zoning.

Accurately reflect social and economic costs of new development at the regional rather than the local scale

In theory, impact fees set at the marginal cost of new development make housing markets more efficient, because they force developers and new residents to internalize the costs imposed on existing residents.[50] In practice, local jurisdictions set their impact fees without taking into account the impacts their housing development (or lack thereof) imposes on neighboring jurisdictions. When cities and counties in the urban core charge high impact fees or use fiscal zoning, that pushes new development to the suburban fringe, which creates more traffic congestion and environmental damage for the entire region. Many outer suburbs arguably have set their impact fees too low from a regional perspective, considering the environmental harms of greenfields development and the inefficiency of underused infrastructure in the urban core.

Mispricing of impact fees by local governments could reflect poor information about the broader social costs, intentional choices to achieve other goals (hostility toward growth, desire to extract concessions from developers during negotiation), or both. State or federal agencies could provide guidelines to help well-meaning localities determine an appropriate range of fees, grounded in data and analysis. To the extent that local governments use impact fees to achieve political aims, creating some system of state or federal review could curb fees that are obviously out of kilter. Some localities routinely ask developers to pay for upgraded services that benefit current residents, not remotely connected to the impacts of new development. Such requests violate at least the spirit of the Nollan-Dolan "rational nexus" ruling, which states that fees should be based on the impact of new development on public services. At the very least, requiring localities to publish an easily accessible schedule of fees—and administer the schedule consistently across development proposals—would improve the transparency and fairness of the system.

Conclusion

Local governments are responsible for providing adequate community infrastructure to support both existing residents and population growth. Cities and counties rely heavily on property taxes to maintain existing infrastructure, while using impact fees to finance expansions that serve new housing. These financing mechanisms raise a number of concerns, including contributing to high housing costs and limited supply in growing regions, while regions with declining populations struggle to adequately maintain existing services. Poor households are effectively priced out of communities with high-quality infrastructure, exacerbating economic and racial segregation.

A number of policy levers could help. Raising the effective price of building housing in greenfields suburban areas would encourage more infill development that makes use of existing infrastructure. Targeted state-level redistribution can address economic and racial disparities in public service quality. Regionwide impact fees and revenue sharing across cities and counties within metro areas would help align incentives between central cities and suburbs. Increased emphasis on regional financing could also improve coordination problems around land use practices—as discussed in chapter 7.

7

Overcoming the Limits of Localism

Tourists visiting Boston love to stroll through Boston Common, enjoying the park's landscaping and historic monuments, or skating on the Frog Pond. On the other side of the Charles River, Cambridge Common is less picturesque and more utilitarian, with softball fields and walking paths. Both spaces have been adapted from their original purpose in the seventeenth century: open grassy fields where nearby townspeople could bring their cattle to graze. At the time that Boston, Cambridge, and many of their New England neighbors were founded, the local common sat at the spatial center of a village economy. People's daily activities occurred within a few miles of their home, because walking and riding on horseback were the only modes of transportation. How Boston decided to allocate its land between homes, farm plots, and a few small shops had little impact on towns located five or ten miles away.

Today, the Boston metropolitan area has over 4 million people, who participate in one regional labor market—but whose land use decisions are made by more than a hundred independent cities and towns. Residents of Concord can travel the eighteen miles from their historically preserved nineteenth-century village center to downtown Boston in less than half an hour by car, or slightly longer by commuter rail. The land use, housing, infrastructure, and tax policy decisions made by each city and town have noticeable spillover effects on their neighbors and on the regional economy. Delegating authority over land use and housing production to local governments made sense when "downtown" meant the village common. Today, our continued deference to local control creates problems.

In theory, local control over public services offers some advantages, especially in a country as large and diverse as the United States. Mayors and city councilors may have better information on what voters in their jurisdiction want than congressional representatives and, by virtue of closer geographic proximity, can be more easily held accountable. In practice, the virtues of localism are less clear. Allowing each city, town, or county to determine how much housing to build (or not build) leads to poor economic, social, and environmental outcomes for metro areas, states, and the country overall. Local political and fiscal incentives are often in direct conflict with regional well-being. Further, local governments vary widely in their resources and institutional capacity, which affects their ability to plan and implement effective policies. Therefore, the quality and quantity of services funded and provided by local government vary widely from place to place.

Several governance changes could enhance the capacity of all local governments to deliver better housing market outcomes to their constituents, while also combating the parochialism that hampers regional and national housing markets. State and federal governments should set clear goals for local governments (standards for well-functioning housing markets), as well as provide financial support and technical assistance. Using federal or state funds to incentivize greater regional cooperation could also improve economic outcomes. Creating financial "sticks" to penalize localities that choose not to comply may be necessary for some determinedly exclusionary places.

Federal subsidies boost housing demand, while states create the legal framework in which local governments operate

Local governments exercise the most direct control over housing markets, particularly land use planning and the housing production process. But state and federal agencies play key roles in providing subsidies and creating a regulatory framework (table 7-1).

The federal government provides subsidies that boost housing demand, especially for homeownership. As discussed in chapters 4 and 5, the federal government gives preferential tax treatment and interest rate subsidies to homeowners, as well as rental vouchers to a small share of low-income renters. These subsidies enable households to spend more on housing than they otherwise would; for instance, encouraging people to purchase larger, more expensive homes. However, the federal government has little direct influence over housing supply. Even federally subsidized housing construction, such as the low-income housing tax credit (LIHTC) program discussed in chapter 4, must be approved through local governments' housing development process. Zoning rules that prohibit construction of market-rate apartments apply equally to subsidized apartments, and the discretionary approval process often creates much higher hurdles for below-market apartments.

Over the decades, federal officials from former U.S. Department of Housing and Urban Development (HUD) secretary George Romney to Senator Cory Booker have discussed the possibility of strategically withholding federal funds from local governments with exclusionary zoning rules.[1] Current federal programs are not well designed to wield leverage over the right places. In HUD's budget, the most likely candidate to use as a fiscal stick is the Community Development Block Grant (CDBG) Program, which provides flexible funds to state and local governments that can be used for housing-related purposes. The U.S. Department of Transportation distributes funds to states, regions, and localities for both roads and public transit. However, both CBDG and transportation funds are distributed according to formulas set by Congress, based on

TABLE 7-1. Federal and state governments have some levers to influence local housing outcomes.
Selected federal and state subsidies and regulations that affect housing markets.

POLICY TYPE	FEDERAL	STATE
Subsidies	Homeownership tax benefits (MID)	Some housing construction and maintenance (rehabilitation and weatherization grants)
	Mortgage interest rate subsidy	
	Low-income rental vouchers	
	Low-income rental construction (LIHTC)	
	Tax exemption for municipal bonds	
Intergovernmental grants	Roads, public transit, water, other infrastructure	Distribute federal grants (LIHTC, CDBG, transit)
	Community development (CDBG)	Schools, transportation
Regulations	Mortgage market regulation	Set parameters for local government authority: land use and taxation
	Environmental regulations (NEPA)	Environmental regulations, building code (above national baseline)
	Manufactured housing code	Regulate landlord-tenant relationships
	Labor requirements (minimum wage, Davis–Bacon)	"Fair share" housing requirements (MA, NJ)
		Some regional planning requirements (CA, OR)
Information sharing	Technical assistance to state/local	Some research and TA
	Convening, best practices, research	

Note: MID (mortgage interest deduction), LIHTC (Low-Income Housing Tax Credit), CDBG (Community Development Block Grant), NEPA (National Environmental Policy Act), TA (technical assistance).

population and other demand proxies. Congressional approval would be needed to rewrite those formulas, giving executive agencies the ability to strategically allocate the funds to influence land use planning and housing production by local governments. Moreover, CDBG funds are heavily weighted toward large cities with higher poverty rates—wealthy suburban communities that have the most problematic zoning receive little direct CBDG money.[2] While the federal government plays an out-sized role in regulating mortgage markets and subsidizing homeownership, it has chosen not to use these tools to achieve broader policy outcomes, like discouraging development in environmentally sensitive areas (chapter 3).

States have substantially more leverage over local governments through two different channels. Critically, states create the legal parameters under which local governments operate, specifying the degree of local authority over land use and defining the set of fiscal tools available to localities (chapter 6). Some states grant their local governments broad powers to adopt and modify zoning and other land use policies, with few restrictions. Other states have granted more limited authority and may require localities to ask state permission before adopting some types of regulatory changes. A somewhat controversial power of state governments is their ability to pre-empt local governments from adopting certain policies; a number of states prohibit localities from adopting local rent regulation or mandatory inclusionary zoning policies. States that want to discourage exclusionary zoning could pre-empt localities from banning apartments, at least in designated areas.[3] Chapter 8 discusses some recent statewide efforts along these lines.

Another channel for state influence over localities is through more strategic redistribution of existing funds. States act as intermediaries in distributing a number of federal funding streams, including LIHTC and some CDBG and transportation funds. As discussed in chapter 6, many states also redistribute their own revenues for K–12 schools. In theory, some of these funds could be used as carrots or sticks to influence local governments' housing production.

There are several ways in which state policy has a direct impact on housing outcomes. Landlord-tenant law is set at the state level, influencing renters' legal protections and the eviction process. Some states have chosen to set higher standards than the federal government for environmental regulation. Given the inadequate response of the federal government in limiting housing growth in climate-risky locations, state efforts could be quite beneficial, if designed thoughtfully. One notable exception is the California Environmental Quality Act, which is widely criticized for giving opponents of new development excessive power to delay or prevent even climate-friendly projects, like bike lanes.[4] Massachusetts and New Jersey have statewide "fair share" laws that (in theory) require all localities to provide some lower-cost housing. State agencies in California and Oregon have several mechanisms to oversee local government efforts in housing planning and production, and are debating whether to expand state influence. The effectiveness of these efforts is discussed in chapter 8.

Local governments wield multiple tools to influence housing outcomes

Local governments have policy tools available that can influence housing demand (to a certain extent) and supply within their jurisdictions. Some of the tools mirror or overlap with those used by federal and state governments (designing tax strategies and subsidies), but several are unique to local governments, notably designing and enforcing land use plans.[5] Each policy area has both a planning and design component (adopting new policies or changing existing ones) and an implementation component (administering and enforcing policies already on the books). The skills and resources required to undertake each of these tasks vary.[6] Localities with tighter capacity (including staff time and expertise) may either choose not to do certain tasks or may struggle to perform them well. In general, developing new policies and regulations is more complex than administering existing policies.

Land use planning is among the most important tools at local governments' disposal to influence housing markets. Cities and counties decide how much land should be allocated to housing, retail, and other commercial uses, or reserved as open space. They determine the process by which land can be developed or redeveloped, as well as the physical dimensions buildings must conform to. Changes to a community's comprehensive plan and zoning code directly affect the quantity, type, and cost of newly built housing. Closely related, localities plan for expansions or upgrades in infrastructure: where to add new bus stops or increase service frequency, which roads need repaving and sidewalks repairing. Infrastructure investments influence the quality of life in surrounding neighborhoods, which is capitalized into housing prices or rents.

As discussed in chapter 6, local governments have a wide range of fiscal tools available to raise revenues for local public services. Each one of these tools requires some planning and design: What is the "right" millage rate for property taxes? Should there be different rates for residential and commercial properties? How large should a homestead exemption be? Administering property taxes consistently and accurately—including updating assessed values to track changes in housing markets—is essential to a locality's fiscal health and can be quite complicated, especially in times and places with volatile housing prices.

Some of the housing policy tasks described in table 7-2 are essential housekeeping duties that every local government must carry out: collecting property taxes and processing deed transfers when homes are sold are universal responsibilities. Beyond that, the housing policies local governments choose to pursue reflect economic conditions often outside their control, as well as the political choices of local residents. Managing new development is a high priority for places experiencing rapid job and population growth, which includes most Sunbelt metros. Cities and counties in regions experiencing slow population and job growth—much of the Midwest and noncoastal Northeast, as well as rural areas—face the challenge of maintaining the quality of exist-

TABLE 7-2. Local governments have tools to influence both housing demand and supply.
Examples of locally administered housing and land use policies.

POLICY AREA	PLANNING AND POLICY DESIGN	ADMINISTER AND ENFORCE POLICIES
Land use	Plan for housing, nonresidential uses, infrastructure	Manage development process, issue permits
Fiscal policy	Set tax rates and fee structure	Collect taxes and fees; update property value assessments
Climate resilience	Develop climate mitigation, adaptation, and emergency response strategies	Upgrade public buildings, administer grants
Building stock management	Update building code	Inspect new development, monitor existing buildings
	Historic preservation	Record property sales, deed transfers, and mortgages
	Develop and manage subsidized housing	
Housing subsidies	Design local subsidies, homelessness outreach	Administer state and federal subsidies (CDBG, vouchers)
	IZ, homebuyer assistance	Compliance with IZ
Tenant protection		Adjudicate landlord-tenant complaints, administer rent regulation

Note: IZ (inclusionary zoning). CDBG (Community Development Block Grant)

ing buildings and infrastructure with an aging and shrinking population. Climate adaptation and mitigation are top priorities for coastal communities from South Florida to New Orleans to Norfolk. Localities that choose to adopt a complex set of regulations and local housing subsidies—such as discretionary development processes, historic preservation, rent regulation, and inclusionary zoning—will then need to devote more resources to administering those policies in future.

In a large, diverse country, local decisionmaking offers some advantages

Delegating oversight for production and maintenance of the nation's housing stock to local governments has some practical advantages. It is hard to envision efficiency gains from requiring the federal government to authorize every new suburban subdivision or home renovation, for instance. Real estate is inherently tied to places, to land and structures. In a country as geographically large as the United States, implementation of housing policy benefits from at least some physical proximity between public officials and the buildings they oversee.

Less tied to the tangible nature of housing, the U.S. federal system can accommodate wide variation in people's preferences over a whole range of government activities. Specifically, what services do voters want their governments to provide, and how much in taxes are they willing to pay for those services? At the national level, disagreement over taxation and government spending often splits along partisan lines, with Republicans generally arguing for lower taxes on high-income individuals and corporations, and less public spending on programs that benefit lower-income people. Given the breadth of voter preferences, any mixture of fiscal policy chosen by the federal government is likely to leave a large number of voters dissatisfied.

At the local level, though, individual cities, towns, and counties can tailor their "bundle" of taxes and public services to fit the preferences of a particular group of voters. Economist Charles Tiebout developed an influential theory that local public finance is more efficient because voters can choose where to live in order to match their preferences, as people sort themselves across localities.[7] Residents of Sumter County, Florida—home of The Villages, an enormous master-planned retirement community—would prefer that their county supervisors concentrate their tax dollars on health care and golf courses. In Parkland, Florida, children under eighteen make up more than one-third of the population, three times the number of older adults.[8] Communities like Parkland have greater resident support for investing in high-quality primary and secondary schools. Tiebout sorting is particularly helpful for understanding location choice across cities and towns within the same metro area. Most households choose their larger region based on job availability but have flexibility within that region to pick a community that meets their lifestyle preferences and fits within their housing budget, including property taxes.[9]

In practice, Tiebout sorting raises concerns about the equity of a world where people choose their neighbors based on purchasing power. A clear implication is that wealthy households can pay more for public services, creating an incentive for them to cluster in the same community while excluding less affluent people. A 1 percent property tax rate assessed on million-dollar homes generates a lot more revenue than the same nominal rate applied to $250,000 homes.

A different argument for devolving service provision to local governments suggests that local officials are more accountable to their voters.[10] The greater probability of in-person encounters between mayors or county supervisors and their constituents should keep local officials well informed about the community's needs and highly motivated to serve them well. No elected official wants to be shouted at in the grocery store.

Yet data from surveys and voter turnout suggest that people are less engaged in local politics than in national debates.[11] Voters are less likely to know their city council member's name than their senator's. Turnout in purely local elections is around half that in federal elections.[12]

Low turnout in local elections means that a small number of voters— who are not necessarily representative of the whole community—are often the deciding factor in who wins. Voters who consistently participate in local elections—and who write angry emails to their elected officials—tend to be people who benefit from the status quo and vehemently oppose any changes. In both local and federal elections, affluent, well-educated white residents are more likely to vote.[13] Elected officials are mostly homeowners themselves, even in majority-renter cities.[14] Long-time homeowners are generally the loudest voices, are the best organized, and have more resources to fight against policies they dislike. By definition, voters in any locality are people who can afford to live there—while people who would benefit most from changes are outside the locality, including future generations.

Policies popular with local voters may harm broader regional or national well-being

Anyone who has listened to a pledge drive on their local public radio station is familiar with the free rider problem. More financial support allows the station to offer better programming, which all listeners presumably want. Yet, for any single listener, it is tempting to let others pick up the bill. Governments face this challenge with a range of public services: how can they convince everyone to chip in a little bit of money, or to put up with some inconvenience, to achieve the greater good for everyone?

Services that are funded or provided by local governments replicate the free rider problem, with local communities standing in for individual taxpayers.[15] Some goods and services are necessary for a regional economy to work, but every local community prefers that some other locality provide. Three key components of a regional economy that often face local pushback include housing for lower-wage workers, transportation infrastructure, and some types of commercial activity.

A metro area's economy functions better when workers at all income levels have someplace to live—when baristas, landscapers, and house-keepers can live within reasonable commuting distance of their jobs.[16] Yet most localities within the metro area would prefer to have middle- and upper-income residents, who live in higher-value homes that bring in more property tax revenues. The fiscal incentives to exclude low-income residents are especially strong for primarily residential communities with small populations; they depend heavily on tax revenues from homes to fund local services, and perceive themselves as having minimal responsibility for the larger region's labor market.

NIMBYism by local governments hinders the development of regional transportation systems. Affluent communities from Georgetown to Beverly Hills have fought against building or expanding public transit, making it difficult to locate rail stations (and sometimes entire lines) where they make the most economic sense.[17] Since the 1970s, the costs of building transportation systems have risen substantially, in part due to the increasing importance of "citizen voice."[18] In some instances, resident opposition has allowed low-income, Black and brown communities to fend off harmful projects and displacement (Greenwich Village and Shaker Heights, Ohio, are good examples). But citizen voice has also been weaponized by wealthy white communities to block infrastructure like public transit that would have benefited lower-income workers. This resistance often results in poor transit access to suburban job centers, limiting employment opportunities for workers who can't afford to own cars. It can also reduce the amount of funds available for regional transit funding.

Local resistance can also complicate achieving a good regional balance between jobs and housing. The fiscal incentives for local governments to approve residential versus nonresidential development vary across states, because of underlying differences in tax structure. In states where cities and counties face restrictions on their ability to increase property taxes but have more flexibility in levying sales taxes, commercial development may be more appealing. On the flip side, small, affluent bedroom suburbs often deny proposals for retail development—

especially the dreaded big-box stores—on the grounds that it will increase traffic.

Misalignment between local and regional well-being exists in every state and metro area, but the problem is worse in regions with a particularly fragmented government, defined as a large number of small population localities.[19] Larger cities and counties tend to have a more diverse housing stock, which accommodates more economic and racial diversity among residents.[20] It is easier for small places to convince themselves that their policies don't matter for regional outcomes, that some other locality will provide moderately priced workforce housing, jobs, and other regionally important infrastructure. Meanwhile, the per capita cost of providing public services is higher in low-density, sprawling metro areas.[21]

Local governments have widely varying capacity to develop and implement policies

The United States has nearly 40,000 general-purpose governments (counties, cities, towns, villages, and boroughs) that are in charge of land use planning. Discussions about urban policy often focus on large, high-profile cities, but those are outliers among U.S. communities. The median incorporated place (census-speak for cities and towns) has around 1,200 residents. Eighty-five percent of incorporated communities have fewer than 10,000 residents.[22] Besides population size, localities vary enormously in their financial resources, size and expertise of staff, and institutional structure. Planning boards often rely on part-time volunteers, who may not have any professional background in land use or housing policy. Any federal program that passes along implementation responsibility to local communities—for instance, requiring cities to revise their zoning codes with more housing-friendly terms—should be mindful of this wide variation in local government capacity, as well as the limits imposed on communities by state governments.

To illustrate a few of the key differences in local government capacity, consider three cities in the Los Angeles metro area (table 7-3). The City of Los Angeles, the second-largest city by population in the United States, employs nearly 400 staff in its planning department, with an annual budget of more than $60 million. They oversee a wide range of plans and policies, including the city's zoning ordinance, comprehensive plan, neighborhood plans, transit-oriented communities, and sustainability, according to the department's extensive website. Los Angeles also has separate departments of building and safety, housing and community investment, neighborhood empowerment, and the housing authority. This size and structure allow the city to employ staff who are specialists at different forms of planning and policy.

Understandably, a city the size of Los Angeles will have a larger and more sophisticated government than smaller communities in the region. But population size alone isn't the only—or even the primary— determinant of local government capacity. Consider two cities in Los Angeles County of very similar population size: San Marino and Commerce. San Marino is a primarily residential suburb, roughly twelve miles northeast of Downtown Los Angeles. With a median household income over $150,000 per year, and a median home value of $1.5 million, it is also one of the wealthiest communities in the region and the country. Eight staff members (nearly all full time) work in the San Marino planning department, which has an annual budget of $1.6 million. The city of Commerce, located about seven miles southeast of Downtown Los Angeles, has a larger nonresidential tax base, including a large outlet mall and an industrial district adjacent to freight rail lines. The population is majority Latino, with a median household income of $42,700, slightly below the metro area median. Commerce's planning department employs four staff, with an annual budget under $700,000.

Beyond the difference in staff head counts, Los Angeles and San Marino employ qualitatively different types of planning staff than Commerce. Commerce's four-person department consists of a director and three code enforcement staff members, who ensure compliance with zoning, building codes, and other regulations. San Marino also employs

TABLE 7-3. All city governments are not created equal.

Variation in local planning department capacity, selected Los Angeles cities.

	LOS ANGELES	COMMERCE	SAN MARINO	L.A. METRO
Population	3.96 million	12,933	13,285	48,974
Household income	$54,400	$42,700	$152,500	$73,567
Home value	$549,800	$357,200	$1,550,100	$561,600
Total permits, 2015–2019	75,435	7	40	200
Planning dept. staff	Approx. 400	4	8	n/a
Planning dept. budget	$60.9 million	$667,000	$1.6 million	n/a

Sources: Los Angeles Controller, 2021, https://lacontroller.org/wp-content/uploads/2019/09/BUDGET-2019-20.pdf; Los Angeles Planning Department, 2021, https://planning.lacity.org/about/department; San Marino Finance, 2021, http://cms9.revize.com/revize/sanmarinoca/Finance/Budgets/Final%20FY19-20%20Adopted%20Budget.pdf; San Marino, 2021, Staff Directory, http://cms9.revize.com/revize/sanmarinoca/government/staff_directory/index.php; Commerce City, 2021, Budget, www.ci.commerce.ca.us/Home/ShowDocument?id=210; and Commerce City, 2021, Staff Directory, www.ci.commerce.ca.us/city-hall/staff-directory/-sortn-SDepts/-sortd-asc.

Note: Population and income from 2018 ACS. L.A. metro column shows median value for all 122 incorporated jurisdictions in the metro area (excluding unincorporated parts of L.A. and Orange County). Planning department staff counts and budgets obtained from city websites (January 2021). Staff counts do not distinguish between part-time and full-time positions.

three code enforcement staff, but nearly half its department staff are planners of varying seniority: jobs primarily oriented toward designing and implementing new policies, not statutory compliance.

There isn't a clear, objective benchmark for how many staff a planning department should employ, so it is hard to say whether Commerce is understaffed or San Marino is overstaffed. Neither jurisdiction has seen much housing growth recently: between 2015 and 2019, Commerce approved permits for seven new homes (total) and San Marino for forty homes. San Marino acknowledges that facilitating growth is less important than preserving its exclusive nature: the city's website states, "Maintaining the high-quality residential character of San Marino is the top priority of the Community Development Department."[23]

The side-by-side comparison of these three communities illustrates how localism and Tiebout sorting can exacerbate racial and economic segregation within a region. While in theory, households can "vote with their feet" to find a community that best fits their preferences, not all households have the same choices. The typical family living in San Marino could afford to live in any community within the Los Angeles metro, but the typical family in Los Angeles or Commerce is effectively barred from living in San Marino—and therefore benefiting from the city's schools, parks, and other public services—because of the high housing costs. Initial resource deficits put small, lower-income communities like Commerce at a systemic disadvantage: they cannot afford to invest in improving public services and place-based amenities that could attract higher-income residents.

Solutions

An effective set of solutions will include financial carrots and sticks to change motivations, as well as support for capacity building where needed. As described in chapter 2, exclusionary zoning creates the worst housing distortions in high-demand places within strong regional labor markets, so these communities ought to be the highest priority for reform efforts. Among all the localities in this group, many genuinely want to provide better housing outcomes for their current residents and support regional needs, but they may not know which policies to change or in what ways. But some communities have highly sophisticated local voters and officials who know exactly what they are doing and have no desire to change. Effective tactics and tools need to recognize these different intents.

Clear policy guidance plus easy-to-access technical assistance would help good-faith actors

Not all the solutions require enormous political challenges or financial investments. Low-hanging fruit would be for HUD (and/or state housing agencies) to provide local governments with clear guidelines on what better policies and better housing outcomes look like. As described in chapter 2, two key goals are zoning rules that allow a diverse range of housing types and a shorter, simpler, more transparent development process. Developing straightforward guidance on how to implement these changes, with examples for different housing market conditions and institutional frameworks, would provide good-faith localities with useable information, without requiring much new funding or creating political confrontations.

Translating general guidance into concrete changes will create challenges for localities with very limited resources and staff capacity. One-person planning departments can't take on responsibility for rewriting their town zoning codes without dropping all existing tasks. Smaller, resource-constrained communities should be able to request advice and technical assistance from HUD, state agencies, or potentially organizations like the National Association of Counties. These organizations could identify clusters of small localities with similar economic and housing market conditions and equivalent institutional capacity to take part in joint training sessions, creating some economies of scale. One important consideration in designing any technical assistance is that communities requesting help shouldn't have to struggle through complex, paperwork-heavy applications. The typical federal grant application requires organizational skills comparable to a CPA, forcing many smaller communities to pay for professional grant-writers just to get a bite of the apple.

Create meaningful financial incentives for regional cooperation in land use planning

Achieving better regional housing outcomes, especially in metros like New York, Boston, Los Angeles, and the Bay Area, will take more than scattered voluntary reforms by a handful of jurisdictions. States and the federal government will need to use financial carrots and sticks to encourage cooperation and coordination among many jurisdictions.

Regional planning is not a new idea: scholars (e.g., Myron Orfield) have been writing about regional coordination on housing, land use, and economic development since the 1990s.[24] And there are some existing structures and mechanisms: metropolitan planning organizations (MPOs) bring together representatives of local governments in large urban areas to develop plans for spending federal transportation funds.[25] MPOs also convene their member communities to discuss housing and land use, but unlike transportation, there is no funding stream attached to housing. One option would be to shift the allocation of existing federal housing programs—such as CDBG and LIHTC—from local and state agencies to MPOs, requiring the region to submit a collective plan in order to unlock the funds. This could be supplemented by creating new competitive grant programs—a top-up for housing, transportation, parks, or other community infrastructure—for MPOs that commit to meeting regional housing production and affordability goals.

Channeling funds for low-income housing through MPOs wouldn't provide much motivation for wealthy, intentionally exclusive communities to change their behavior. Small, wealthy suburbs don't currently receive much federal funding for housing or community development and would likely choose to forgo funds rather than implement zoning changes they don't like to build subsidized housing they don't want.

Any federal or state intervention that seriously intends to combat exclusionary behavior should be prepared to use sturdy financial "sticks"—withholding funds for services that wealthy communities truly want, like K–12 schools or road maintenance.

Shifting responsibility from local governments up to state and federal agencies would create some risks. Federal priorities can swing abruptly when presidential administrations turn over, especially when power changes across parties. Most state governments have not directly engaged with land use or housing supply in the past, so they would need to build up some state-level capacity. The political dynamics between state legislatures and local governments can be fraught—especially the relationship between Republican-dominated legislatures and Democratic mayors of large cities. As discussed in chapter 8, housing politics are not neatly aligned with traditional partisan divides; shifting to more state involvement has the potential to improve housing outcomes, relative to the status quo, but it is not without risk.

Conclusion

Our highly decentralized system of local control over land use contributes to regional housing shortages and environmentally unsustainable development patterns, and it exacerbates racial and economic segregation. But localism is deeply entrenched in American democracy, which makes it very difficult to change. State and federal interventions could help, by supporting voluntary reform of well-intentioned communities and encouraging more regional coordination. The policies likely to be most effective at changing exclusionary behavior will also generate the most political opposition from local governments. A few states and cities have assembled political coalitions to support land use reforms—as explored in chapter 8.

8

Build Political Coalitions around Better Policies

Consider the topics that routinely get airtime during a presidential campaign: jobs and the macroeconomy, health care, and immigration occupy prime real estate in candidates' stump speeches and on the debate stage. If housing gets a mention at all, it is generally in the form of a platitude about homeownership being part of the American dream.[1] George W. Bush spoke about an "ownership society," and Barack Obama—who took office in the midst of a national foreclosure crisis—pushed for "sustainable homeownership."[2] The inadequacy of rental subsidies, whether housing supply is keeping up with demand, the relationship between housing markets and climate change—these topics rarely get mentioned by candidates running for national office. Although there is plenty of disagreement around how to address issues like health care, it is impossible to solve problems that we aren't talking about.

But there are some promising signs. During the 2020 presidential campaign cycle, nearly all the Democratic candidates developed policy proposals aimed at improving housing affordability, specifically calling out zoning as a contributing factor to high housing costs.[3] The role of zoning in exacerbating economic and racial segregation even made some headlines during the general election campaign, with the then president Donald Trump falsely alleging that the former vice president Joseph Biden wanted to "abolish the suburbs" through more vigorous enforcement of fair housing laws.[4]

These episodes represent a significant increase in visibility. High-profile candidates drawing attention to housing raises the salience among voters at large and reflects a growing awareness that poorly functioning housing markets are not just problems for local or state governments. The economic, environmental, and social consequences of bad housing outcomes extend well beyond city or even state borders. Many localities and regions are struggling to come up with solutions to very similar problems—efforts that would benefit from more conversations and collaboration across places.

The greater visibility of housing on the national stage, along with some notable state and local policy reforms, offers some hope for breaking out of long-standing bad outcomes. But reform efforts have to contend with deeply entrenched financial and political interests. And support is likely to come from unusual coalitions that cross partisan lines—both a potential strength and a limitation of the burgeoning YIMBY (yes in my backyard) movement.

State and local success stories on prohousing reforms

Over the past few years, a handful of state and local governments have successfully passed policies that make it easier to build a diversity of housing types—from duplexes to rowhouses to apartment buildings—in areas where they were previously illegal. Collectively, these reforms have begun to raise questions about the dominant practice of single-family-exclusive zoning. What exactly that means is important both conceptually and linguistically. Single-family-exclusive zoning prohibits all housing structures *except* single-family detached homes. The type of reforms discussed in this chapter are sometimes referred to collectively as "ending single-family zoning," a phrase that often invites confusion. In practice, zoning reforms would make it legal to build other specified structures (duplexes, accessory dwelling units [ADUs], etc.) in neighborhoods where they are currently prohibited. None of the proposed reforms would restrict the ability to build new single-family-detached homes, or call for the demolition of existing homes.

The people and organizations behind state and local zoning reform efforts vary from place to place. While there are a number of national organizations devoted to housing policy advocacy in various forms—such as Habitat for Humanity and the National Low Income Housing Coalition—there is not yet a national organization or network associated with zoning reform. Some zoning reform advocates have embraced the term "YIMBY," but the term itself is not uncontroversial. Indeed, one lesson emerging from local campaigns is that the words used for framing and communication are quite important and should be tailored to local context. "Legalizing apartments" is a more precise, less ominous framing than "ending single-family zoning."[5] Similarly, how the policies are designed and which existing political actors can be mobilized in support vary across places.

To date, cities and states have proposed three types of zoning reforms (some efforts include multiple approaches): legalizing small-scale housing (sometimes called "missing middle" or "gentle density"); increasing housing capacity near public transit and commercial corridors; and allowing owners of single-family homes to create secondary apartments, known as ADUs.[6] While zoning reforms have been particularly salient in high-cost coastal markets, they are also showing up in less obvious places (table 8-1). The policy landscape is changing rapidly; this list presents a partial inventory as of April 2021. The coalitions behind some of these efforts offer insight into the underlying political interests and tensions.

Minneapolis made headlines in December 2018 when the city council voted to adopt a new comprehensive plan that called for legalizing duplexes and triplexes in all residential areas.[7] The city's new plan also in-

TABLE 8-1. Attempts at zoning reform are popping up across the United States.
Selected state and local zoning reform bills, 2018–2021.

REFORM TYPE	CITY/STATE	YEAR
Legalize "missing middle"	Minneapolis	2018
	Sacramento, Berkeley	2021
	Oregon	2019
	Nebraska	2020
	Virginia	2020
Upzone near transit	Massachusetts	2021
	California	2018–current
	Connecticut	2021
Legalize ADUs	California, Washington	
Other	Utah	2019
	North Carolina	2019

Sources: Michael Andersen, "Here's Oregon's New Bill to Re-legalize 'Missing Middle' Homes Statewide," January 10, 2019, www.sightline.org/2019/01/10/ore gon-missing-middle-homes-hb-2001; David Garcia, "ADU Update: Early Lessons and Impacts of California's State and Local Policy Changes" (Berkeley, CA: Terner Center, December 21, 2017); https://nebraskalegislature.gov/Floor Docs/106/PDF/Intro/LB794.pdf; https://le.utah.gov/~2019/bills/static/SB0034 .html; www.ncleg.gov/Sessions/2019/Bills/House/PDF/H675v4.pdf; and www.nc leg.gov/Sessions/2019/Bills/House/PDF/H675v7.pdf.

creased allowable densities near light rail stations and reduced minimum parking requirements, although neither of these provisions drew nearly as much public comment. The successful vote followed several years of intensive organizing and advocacy by elected leaders—City Council President Lisa Bender and Mayor Jacob Frey were both vocal supporters of the effort—and volunteer community groups, such as the new Neighbors for More Neighbors coalition. Advocates for zoning reform framed the issue largely in terms of racial justice, pointing out the persistently large disparities in income, wealth, and homeownership rates between white, Black, and Native American households in the Twin Cities—a touchy issue in a city known for progressive politics and "Minnesota nice" attitudes. The campaign used redlining maps from the 1930s to show how neighborhoods that had been systematically excluded from federally subsidized mortgages still had the highest concentration of Black and Native households and among the lowest incomes in the city.[8]

In June 2019, Oregon's state legislature passed an even more groundbreaking law (HB 2001) that pushed back against single-family-exclusive zoning throughout the state. The bill was shepherded by the house speaker, Tina Kotek, and passed with bipartisan support.[9] Oregon's law contains a package of zoning changes: cities with more than 10,000 residents must allow duplexes in residential areas, while cities over 25,000 must allow triplexes, fourplexes, townhouses, and "cottage clusters."[10] The legislation includes incentives for small multifamily properties to include some units that are reserved for low-income households.

Similar to Minneapolis's efforts, the successful passage followed years of advocacy and coalition-building. Key coalition members included building trade unions, environmental groups, nonprofit affordable housing developers such as Habitat for Humanity, as well as for-profit housing developers. To pull these disparate interests together, the zoning reform bill was paired with other bills addressing housing concerns, notably including statewide rent regulation and tenant protections.[11] Traditional affordable housing advocates have expressed concerns that upzoning could lead to more high-end apartments being built in low-income neighborhoods, contributing to displacement among existing renters—an issue we will come back to later in the chapter. The bill also drew opposition from homeowners in the expensive Eastmoreland community (one of the first areas in the Portland metro to ban attached housing), the Eugene City Council, and the Oregon League of Cities.

When it comes to state efforts to influence local land use policies, California is in a league of its own—although with somewhat mixed results.[12] State senator Scott Weiner launched one of the earliest and most ambitious attempts at statewide zoning reform in December 2018, with the introduction of a bill to allow multifamily buildings up to five stories near transit stations. The initial bill (SB 827) was killed in committee but was reintroduced in modified form the following year (SB 50). While SB 50's main focus was on relaxing zoning near transit and in job-rich areas, it also contained provisions to allow fourplexes as-of-right—without requiring discretionary approval from local residents—in residential areas statewide.

Unsurprisingly, SB 50 drew intense opposition from legislators who represent affluent, low-density suburban districts in both the Bay Area and Southern California.[13] Local governments also dug in their heels against the idea of ceding control over zoning and development to the state (see chapter 7). Supporters of the bill included California YIMBY, a prohousing lobbying group in Sacramento, as well as the California Association of Realtors. Environmental organizations and housing advocacy groups were split on the measure. The Natural Resources Defense Council, California League of Conservation Voters, Habitat for Humanity, and United Ways of California all supported the bill, while the Sierra Club of California and several tenants' unions opposed it. As in Oregon, some groups expressed concerns over whether upzoning would lead to redevelopment of lower-cost apartments.[14] SB 50 underwent numerous revisions in committee, before finally losing in a floor vote on January 31, 2020.

Although SB 50 was the most high profile statewide housing reform bill, the California legislature has approved several other substantive zoning reforms in recent years. The state now allows homeowners to build two ADUs per lot in single-family zones, effectively circumventing local rules banning subdivision of lots and multiple homes. Procedural reforms make it easier for localities to fast-track proposals to build low-income housing.[15]

East Coast states lag in the current wave of zoning reform, despite many metro areas having similarly expensive housing. In early 2021, the Massachusetts legislature approved an economic development bill that will require communities with transit stations to create multifamily zoning districts. The bill was passed with bipartisan support and signed by the state's Republican governor, Charlie Baker.[16] Connecticut considered a similar bill in April 2021, before passing a less ambitious version.[17] In 2020, Virginia Delegate Ibrahim Samirah introduced a bill to legalize duplexes statewide; the bill did not make it out of committee.[18] While housing affordability is a less contentious issue in the Midwest, Plains, and Mountain West states, some statewide bills have also been proposed in Texas, Nebraska, and Utah.[19] Both the geographic breadth and the lack of partisan alignment are unusual, and noteworthy.

Positions on housing policies don't align neatly with partisan positions

Unusually for today's hyperpartisan climate, voters' and elected officials' views about housing policy—especially zoning—do not align neatly along traditional partisan or ideological lines. At least three major arguments are commonly used to motivate zoning reform. First, by limiting housing supply and driving up housing costs, overly restrictive zoning hinders the efficiency of regional labor markets, making it difficult for employers to attract and retain workers. Second, constraining housing growth near job centers and transit pushes new development toward low-density, car-dependent suburbs, which is harmful to the environment and to public health, and forces lower-wage workers into long commutes. Third, exclusionary zoning by affluent, mostly white communities entrenches racial and economic segregation.

The first argument about economic efficiency resonates with probusiness interests who typically align with the Republican Party. A corollary point raised by libertarian-leaning groups is that zoning represents intrusive government control over the property rights of individual landowners. That is, owners of existing single-family houses cannot convert their basements into an income-generating ADU, or redevelop the property into apartments, if zoning prohibits it. The second and third arguments appeal to voters who are concerned with climate change and racial equity, who are more likely to align with the Democratic Party. The potential for bipartisan support is not just theoretical. The list of elected officials who have spoken openly about the need for zoning reform includes Republicans—Governor Charlie Baker of Massachusetts and former San Diego mayor Kevin Falconer—as well as Democrats like Senator Elizabeth Warren and Minneapolis mayor Jacob Frey.[20]

Opposition to zoning reform—or alternatively, support for the status quo—is easy to find in both parties. The regions where restrictive zoning is most widespread—coastal California, Seattle, Boston, New York, and Washington, DC—lean heavily Democratic in national, state, and local elections. It has become a trope that affluent Democratic homeowners in these regions decorate their front yards with signs supporting the Black Lives Matter movement while decrying any proposal to build apartments in their own neighborhoods (figure 8-1). Progressive NIMBYs may be the new "limousine liberals."

Left-leaning voters use a variety of rationales to oppose zoning reform. Some claim that dense housing—even in transit-rich, centrally located areas—is environmentally unfriendly: replacing trees and lawns with apartment buildings makes neighborhoods "less green" visually. Many Democratic-voting constituencies also express hostility toward real estate developers; the idea that relaxing zoning would enhance developers' profits is one of the most commonly cited concerns. Antipathy toward for-profit developers is frequently invoked by long-standing homeowners—exactly the same people whose homes have appreciated substantially due to zoning protections, and who receive large federal tax subsidies (discussed in chapter 5).

The prohousing movement has a somewhat tenuous and uneasy relationship with advocacy groups that represent low-income, Black, and Latino renters. While they share some overlapping goals, there are core differences in their preferred policy outcomes. Groups pushing for zoning reform want to enable more development of market-rate apartments (without subsidies or income restrictions) as well as making it easier to build subsidized rental housing. Renter advocates want more subsidized housing and stronger legal protection for tenants (sometimes including rent regulation), but are wary of market-rate development.

FIGURE 8-1. Housing Twitter on the progressive NIMBY conundrum.

Darrell Owens
@IDoTheThinking

···

The city emblem of Berkeley, California should be a $2 million dollar bungalow with a BLM sign in a neighborhood with no Black people.

1:29 PM · Mar 20, 2021 · Twitter Web App

144 Retweets   **26** Quote Tweets   **1,819** Likes

Source: Darrell Owens (@IDoTheThinking), Twitter, March 20, 2021, https://twitter.com/IDoTheThinking/status/1373325867103911944.

Pushing The Needle
@pushtheneedle

···

Classic Seattle Liberal

12:47 PM · Mar 21, 2021 · Twitter for iPhone

Source: Pushing the Needle (@pushtheneedle), Twitter, March 21, 2021, https://twitter.com/pushtheneedle/status/1373677679975694338.

In many high-cost metros, new market-rate housing has been disproportionately concentrated in moderate-income communities, which
is perceived as contributing to displacement.[21] An emerging strand of
academic research suggests that more new construction reduces nearby
rents and can lessen displacement pressures—but wonky economics
papers aren't terribly effective tools in political debates.[22] The type of
broad, citywide upzonings that prohousing groups advocate are extremely rare in the United States—or too new to have yielded visible
changes yet, as in Minneapolis and Oregon—so there is very little evidence to analyze.[23]

Beyond concrete policy disagreements, a long history of racial discrimination by the real estate industry and heavy-handed public interventions in Black and Latino communities—from urban renewal
and highway construction in the 1950s to police violence today—have
created deep levels of distrust in both the government and the private
sector. As Conor Dougherty notes, the early YIMBY movement in the
Bay Area was dominated by young, college-educated, white "tech bros,"
who failed to build alliances with racially diverse, long-standing housing advocates.[24] Some groups that advocate for zoning reform and more
housing—including Minneapolis's Neighbors for More Neighbors—have
strategically chosen not to use the YIMBY label because of the perceived
baggage attached.[25]

Political support for other housing policies aligns somewhat more
consistently with partisan affiliation. Democratic voters and elected
officials tend to support more spending for subsidies, including housing vouchers. The low-income housing tax credit (LIHTC) program, the
primary below-market production program, has remarkably strong
bipartisan support in Congress, in part because of the range of interest
groups that benefit from it (discussed more later in the chapter). Both
LIHTC and household-based rental assistance are more market-oriented
programs than traditional public housing, boosting their appeal to
Republicans. As a tax credit, LIHTC is administered by the Treasury
Department, rather than the U.S. Department of Housing and Urban

Development (HUD). In recent years, some left-leaning Democratic officials have expressed interest in stronger tenant protections and rent regulation, positions that are largely unpopular with Republicans.[26] Although homeownership subsidies in the federal tax code accrue mostly to higher-income households, it is notable that a Republican-led Congress substantially shrank these subsidies in the 2017 Tax Cuts and Jobs Act.[27]

More interest groups are financially invested in the status quo than in reform

Existing housing policies have created "winners" who are financially invested in keeping things as they are. Restrictive local zoning, federal tax policy, and car-oriented transportation subsidies generate and protect wealth for upper-middle-income homeowners—an important voting bloc in local, state, and federal elections.[28] Various parts of housing policy also have support from real estate industry groups, although some of these relationships are more nuanced than commonly acknowledged.

Breaking down market segments within the real estate industry illustrates these nuances. The National Association of Home Builders, the Mortgage Bankers Association, the National Association of Realtors, and their various state affiliates are primarily oriented around homeownership. While their members would benefit from regulatory changes that make it faster and easier to build for-sale homes—like a streamlined, more transparent development process—they have less to gain from zoning reforms that legalize multifamily rental housing. Their counterparts in the rental market, the National Multifamily Housing Council and National Apartment Association, represent organizations that develop, own, and operate rental housing. Apartment developers have the most to gain from zoning reform and have provided financial support to a number of prohousing advocacy groups. On the other hand, companies that own and operate rental properties in markets where zoning limits new development are able to charge higher rents, so are less anxious to lower the barriers to competition—very similar to the motives of individual homeowners in those markets. There are also some large, well-capitalized, well-connected development companies that choose to operate exclusively in tightly regulated markets because smaller developers can't compete.[29]

Some national organizations advocate on behalf of low-income renters, although most groups have lower public profiles than real estate industry affiliates. The LIHTC program has developed an entire ecosystem of nonprofit organizations that support, and earn revenues from, its complex financing. They vary in size and political influence, from large national groups like the Local Initiatives Support Corporation and Enterprise Community Partners to small, neighborhood-based community development corporations.[30] Public agencies that administer housing vouchers and public housing are represented by the National Association of Housing and Redevelopment Officials and the Council of Large Public Housing Authorities. These organizations primarily use their platforms to request more federal support for existing subsidy programs, and they can be reluctant to acknowledge limitations of these programs, such as the high per-unit cost of LIHTC and housing quality issues in some public housing developments. At least to date, there is no organized lobby around housing subsidies that simply give people money to pay their rent, such as a universal basic income or renter tax credit.

Some cities have tenants' unions or similar organizations that advocate for stronger legal protections for renters. These tend to be locally based in high-cost cities, with little presence in state or national policy conversations, although the COVID-19 pandemic has drawn more attention to their work.[31] As discussed earlier, tenants' rights advocates and zoning reform advocates are not consistently aligned on their policy demands, despite their members having at least some shared economic interests.

All branches and levels of government offer some path to housing policy reforms

The current wave of interest in zoning reform has mostly pushed for changes through legislative bodies (city councils and state legislatures). Achieving legislative victory requires winning support from at least a majority of elected officials in each body—and in some cases a super-majority (Massachusetts town meetings). In many places, that will be a difficult bar to clear: neither elected officials nor their most vocal constituents are low-income renters.

The public process associated with legislative change is often anti-small-d-democratic. Most city councils and state legislatures hold public sessions to hear testimony before voting on bills. Getting on the docket often requires waiting for hours on a weeknight to testify in person (pre-COVID) or navigating online registration systems and web-based hearings on Zoom. The experience itself, speaking in public on the record in front of sometimes hostile audiences, can be daunting. In the relatively small number of cases where we have surveys or polls of broader public opinion, it is not obvious that antihousing interests represent a majority rather than a very vocal minority.[32] In theory, putting proposals to a voter referendum (where referenda are allowed under state law) could elicit input from a wider, more diverse set of voters. In practice, low voter turnout in state and local elections makes this difficult. But more widespread polling might give elected officials better information and political cover to support policies with widespread support and concentrated opposition.

An alternate strategy is to pursue reform through the judicial branch, especially when current policies are clearly tied to civil rights violations and racial segregation. The most famous example is a series of rulings by the New Jersey Supreme Court, known as the Mount Laurel doctrine, which asserted that all municipalities had an obligation to contribute a "fair share" of the region's affordable housing.[33] Following decades of legal fights between wealthy suburbs and the state, New Jersey has established a statewide Council on Affordable Housing that oversees local compliance with affordable housing mandates. Federal fair housing laws provide similar grounds to challenge exclusionary zoning, although cases like Westchester County, New York, show that wealthy suburbs will fight court-ordered changes for decades, at enormous expense to taxpayers.[34] Lawsuits have also brought about changes to funding formulas for public schools in states from California to Texas (chapter 6). Similar arguments could be made about disparate access to essential public services in majority Black and Latino communities. In California, the Housing Accountability Act provides grounds to "sue the suburbs" for failing to approve housing proposals that are allowed on paper under the city's zoning.[35]

But legal challenges cut both ways. As California's decades-long experience with the California Environmental Quality Act demonstrates, creating avenues for citizens to bring lawsuits against harmful development also opens the door for NIMBYs to stop projects with broad public benefit (chapter 6). Pursuing housing policy changes through the courts, rather than the legislative process, may inflame tempers and further entrench opponents. Both the Mount Laurel and the Westchester cases illustrate that successfully winning lawsuits against wealthy, determined suburban homevoters can cost a lot of money and take a very long time, without curing the underlying problem.

Executive agencies at both the state and local level may have some ability to improve policies without requiring legislative approval, depending on the existing legal framework and budget. Oregon and California already assign state agencies a role in overseeing land use, giving them room to strengthen enforcement of existing policies, like California's Regional Housing Needs Assessment.[36] City planning and building departments often have some wiggle room in interpreting zoning and building codes. At the very least, they could improve the transparency and efficiency of their internal development processes, such as tracking how many projects require a waiver of existing zoning rules, or monitoring the time needed to grant approvals.

Division of responsibility for land use and housing policies across all three levels of government means that policy reforms must happen at all three levels—and with better coordination of policies across levels of government—to achieve meaningfully better housing outcomes (table 8-2).

Local governments hold the primary authority to reform zoning and other land use regulations that are currently limiting housing supply in the places where people most want to live. But state and federal governments can use their financial resources to change local governments' incentives and provide clear guidance and technical assistance, especially for resource-constrained localities. The widespread climate implications of where housing does and does not get built provide ample rationale for state and federal engagement in what has traditionally been considered a local concern. Federal investments in a stronger safety net for low-income households, and wealth-building mechanisms outside homeownership, would help alleviate some of the political pressures that distort local housing policies.

The main obstacle to better housing outcomes is not lack of knowledge about policy recommendations. Persuading elected officials and voters to support needed policy changes is hard, because these choices all involve complex tradeoffs—exactly the debates that arise at community meetings across the country. How can communities accommodate population and job growth, while preserving open space and existing neighborhood amenities? Will "the market" build housing that moderate-income families can afford, or only "luxury" housing for rich people? How should local governments balance the competing claims of older, long-term homeowners and younger, newly arrived (or yet-to-arrive) renters? What role should public policy play in regulating, promoting, or subsidizing homes?

These are not just technical problems for city planners and real estate developers, or theoretical conundrums for academics. Fundamentally, they are political issues that weigh up competing claims between different constituencies, including the thorny question of whether some

TABLE 8-2. An action plan to fix America's housing systems.
Policy reforms needed by federal, state, and local governments.

GOAL	POLICY RECOMMENDATIONS	GOVT. LEVEL
Increase quantity and diversity of housing; reduce housing costs in high-opportunity places	Legalize rowhouses, duplexes, and apartment buildings	Local
	Make housing development process simpler and more transparent	Local
	Create financial incentives for better housing outcomes	State, federal
Shrink household carbon footprints; reduce financial exposure to high-climate risk places	Allow more housing near job centers and public transit	Local
	Remove barriers to mixed residential-commercial development	Local
	Increase taxes on driving and improve noncar transportation	Federal, state, local
	Accurately price climate risk into property insurance and mortgage loans	Federal
Improve access to decent-quality, stable housing	Provide income supplements and housing vouchers to poor people	Federal
	Improve effectiveness and efficiency of federal housing subsidies	Federal
	Revise building codes and zoning that restrict low-cost rental housing	State, local
Improve financial security for lower-income households; reduce racial wealth gap	Subsidize asset-building for low- and moderate-income families	Federal
	Encourage short-term liquid savings for all households	Federal
	Reform federal tax subsidies for homeownership	Federal
Invest in efficient, climate-friendly community infrastructure; improve services in low-income communities	Share revenues and infrastructure costs regionally	Local, state, metro
	Tax expensive land and allow higher-density infill development	Local, state
	Allow local governments fiscal flexibility	State
Improve regional housing and labor market outcomes	Set clear guidelines for good housing market outcomes	Federal, state
	Use federal and state funds to incentivize regional cooperation	Federal, state
	Offer technical assistance to resource-constrained local governments	Federal, state

people's financial interests or aesthetic preferences matter more than other people's access to basic shelter.

Solutions

Housing policy reforms, like all other policy changes, are most likely to emerge from successful political organizing efforts, including mobilizing voters and building coalitions. Some institutional changes within existing federal and state agencies could improve policies within the regulatory framework. And the prohousing movement would benefit from articulating a strong, positive vision for the future that could inform political communications.

Create space for land use and renter protections within the federal government

Land use literally has no home within the federal government and most state governments. The three federal agencies that are topically nearest to urban land use are HUD, the U.S. Department of Transportation (DOT), and the Environmental Protection Agency (EPA). Looking at the organizational structure of these agencies, there is no program or department with responsibility or expertise in land use. Under both Democratic and Republican administrations, HUD has periodically expressed concern over how land use regulation impacts housing affordability, but the issue has never been assigned to a particular office. Within HUD, the office for Policy Development and Research has led on several related efforts: George W. Bush's administration established a Regulatory Barriers Clearinghouse; the Obama administration developed the Affirmatively Furthering Fair Housing rule; and the Trump administration established the White House Council on Eliminating Regulatory Barriers to Affordable Housing.[37] HUD employs plenty of economists, lawyers, and planners, but not specifically experts on land use and zoning. DOT and EPA have similar gaps.

Bureaucracies spend effort on policy areas for which they have regulatory authority and where they administer spending programs. Currently, land use doesn't meet either of these criteria at the federal level. Creating designated offices within appropriate agencies, staffed by career civil servants with relevant expertise—depending on the agency, a mix of economists, lawyers, planners, and engineers—would encourage consistent integration of land use considerations into federal policy. Establishing land use offices within multiple federal agencies could be duplicative, or it could encourage approaching the problem from complementary angles. For instance, within HUD the emphasis might be on how zoning affects housing supply, affordability, and racial segregation—all questions well within HUD's mission statement. DOT should consider how zoning and existing land uses affect the usage and return on investments in federally funded transit projects (e.g., how many people live or work within walking distance of subway, light rail, and bus systems). At EPA, climate scientists should focus on how land use affects natural resource consumption and greenhouse gas emissions, discussed in chapter 3. Other federal agencies whose missions have clear overlap with land use include the Federal Housing Finance Agency (mortgage availability and pricing), the U.S. Department of Agriculture (rural land), and the U.S. Department of the Interior (federally owned properties).

A similar argument could be made for the Consumer Financial Protection Bureau to create an office to monitor private rental housing markets. While most landlord-tenant laws in the United States are regulated at the state level, the federal government could play a more active role in developing model lease contracts, serving as a clearinghouse for tenant complaints, and conducting or funding research on housing quality, including making homes more climate resilient. Other developed countries have more prominent federal oversight of private lease contracts, which can provide more consistency and transparency for both renters and property owners.[38] The growth of large corporate landlords whose portfolios cross state boundaries is an argument that state governments alone cannot effectively regulate private rental housing.[39]

As long as there is no one in the federal government whose full-time job is to improve land use or rental housing outcomes, we are unlikely to see better policies.

Elect more renters

Renters and homeowners have at least one fundamental difference in how they perceive the world: homeowners have locked in the largest part of their monthly housing costs for the foreseeable future, while renters' housing costs adjust frequently. (Property taxes can rise along with home prices. The small share of U.S. homeowners with adjustable-rate mortgages do see some variation in payments when interest rates change.) Long-term homeowners in particular often have very little sense of how expensive it is for newcomers to join their community; their guesses of prevailing rents are anchored to outdated information. Several of the 2021 Democratic candidates for New York City mayor estimated the average price of homes in Brooklyn to be around $100,000— well below the actual figure of $900,000.[40] The trope that millennials could afford to buy homes if only they cut out wasteful spending on Starbucks and avocado toast ignores the reality that housing costs have risen substantially faster than the overall rate of inflation for several decades.[41]

The fact that pro-homeownership bias is so deeply baked into every facet of policy is less surprising when we consider how underrepresented renters are among elected officials at every level of government.[42] Every U.S. president in the past 100 years has owned his home. Large supermajorities of sitting senators, representatives, governors, and state legislators own their homes. Even among mayors of majority-renter big cities, renters are a tiny share of elected officials (figure 8-2). Quite simply, renters do not have a voice in government.

The lack of partisan competition in local elections makes it difficult to push back against the status quo. Changing the default options—land use policies that favor detached homes over apartments, transportation policies favoring driving over mass transit, walking and cycling—will

FIGURE 8-2. Renters are scarce among local elected officials.
Homeownership status of mayors and city councilors.

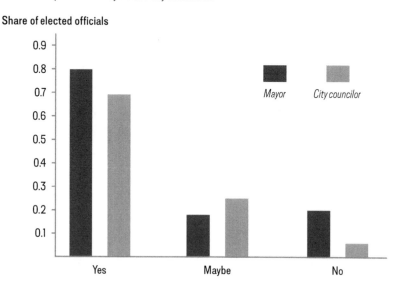

Share of elected officials

Source: Katherine Einstein, Joseph Ornstein, and Maxwell Palmer, "Who Represents the Renters?" (working paper, 2021), http://chriswarshaw.com/lpe_conference/EinsteinOrnsteinPalmer_Homeowners.pdf.

require large-scale shifts in the mindset of elected officials. Even election rules are stacked in favor of long-term, less mobile residents, who are more likely to be homeowners: voters who change addresses more frequently face the burden of updating their voter registration (and voter ID) and locating their new polling place in advance of elections.

Keep YIMBYism bipartisan (or nonpartisan)

Given today's extreme partisan polarization, there are advantages to the YIMBY movement remaining unaffiliated with either political party. The varied rationales in favor of zoning reform makes it possible to motivate the same policy proposal based on economic efficiency, racial equity, or climate benefits, depending on target audiences. Because the YIMBY movement has so far been quite decentralized, made up of local and state organizations, these chapters have been able to frame and motivate their work tailored to the local context. Even some of the federal legislation that has so far been introduced has managed to line up sponsors from both sides of the aisle. Examples include the YIMBY Act, sponsored by Senator Todd Young (R-IN) with Democratic cosponsors.[43] Senator Amy Klobuchar (D-MN) and Senator Rob Portman (R-OH) have introduced a bill to create local planning grants.[44]

Redefine and update the American dream for the twenty-first century

To implement more economically, environmentally, and socially beneficial housing policies, we need to open Americans' hearts and minds to a broader version of the American dream.

Our common ideal of the American dream is stuck in the 1950s. A nuclear family owning a detached home with a yard in economically and racially homogeneous, car-dependent suburbs no longer describes the majority of American households. Single-person households are the fastest-growing group, driven in large part by an aging population. Multigenerational households are also gaining ground to allow caregiving for both children and older family members. The goal of owning a low-density, detached home isn't financially feasible for many young workers, nor is it environmentally sustainable for a growing population. Millennials and younger adults are much more racially diverse than prior generations; if historic gaps in homeownership and household wealth continue, the United States is likely to see substantial declines in homeownership rates over the next twenty years.

People need a positive vision to aspire to. Politicians from both parties, trade groups from financially vested industries, the entertainment and marketing industries (see HGTV) largely still default to outdated images of the American dream (although ads for homebuying are more likely to feature Black and Latino families than in previous decades). Purchasing a detached home is seen not just as one among a range of lifestyle choices, it is conflated with achieving financial stability and adulthood—casting all other choices as failures.

Conclusion

Change is hard. People grow attached to their homes and neighborhoods as they are now—or as they were in the past. Elected officials are
comfortable working within the existing policy framework. Even for
people who struggle under the existing regime, the prospect of change
can be frightening: things can always get worse. Behavioral economists
have taught us that people are particularly averse to losses: our brains
are hardwired to hold onto what we have, even if that means forgoing
a chance to reach better outcomes. Loss aversion is apparent in every
community meeting about new development: debates focus much more
on the costs that might occur with change—more traffic, more noise,
demands on schools—than the costs associated with the status quo.

But our current housing systems create enormous costs, disproportionately borne by vulnerable populations. Low-income families experience constant financial stress, trying to afford the rent on decent-quality
housing in neighborhoods that offer economic opportunity for themselves and their children. Low-density, car-dependent growth on the
urban fringe continues to damage the planet, even while older central
cities struggle to maintain public services for a shrinking population.
Persistent racial and economic segregation, and the unresponsiveness
of elected officials to the needs of their constituents, undermine faith
in our democratic systems. Our broken systems of land use planning,
housing production, social insurance, and public finance contribute to
all of these poor outcomes.

The interconnectedness of these policy systems makes it difficult to
solve one piece at a time. Homeowners' heavy dependence on the equity
in their homes as their main financial asset encourages them to cling to
overly restrictive zoning. Local governments' reliance on property taxes
to fund public services incentivizes policies that exacerbate racial and
economic segregation, which in turn allows high-income households
to live in comfortable bubbles, insulated from day-to-day contact with
poor people.

Our elected officials—whether on the campaign trail or in office—have been reluctant to ask broad swaths of voters to make sacrifices for the greater good. Climate change offers perhaps the clearest example: slowing greenhouse gas emissions will require Americans to give up some daily habits they enjoy (large homes and SUVs) or pay more to keep their current lifestyle. But on the national stage, candidates focus only on the upsides: creating well-paying green jobs appeals to more voters than paying higher parking fees. Even outsider candidates like Tom Steyer and Michael Bloomberg—candidates with slim chances of winning who profess a strong commitment to climate action—didn't level with voters on how mitigation and adaptation will affect their daily lives.

Reforming our current housing and land use systems will shake up the groups of winners and losers. Rolling back exclusionary zoning across enough localities to improve regional housing production and affordability will require affluent homeowners to accept changes in their neighborhoods, and local governments will likely have to cede some control over land use policy to state or federal governments—or pay financial penalties. Providing adequate rental assistance to all low-income households and ensuring decent-quality infrastructure to all communities will require well-off voters to pay more in taxes. Elected officials, from mayors to governors to the president, are understandably reluctant to deliver unpleasant news to their constituents. But the only way we can move toward a better future is to present Americans with an honest, direct assessment of our current problems and concrete proposals for reform.

Notes

1. Jenny Schuetz, Vicki Been, and Ingrid Ellen, "Neighborhood Effects of Concentrated Mortgage Foreclosures," *Journal of Housing Economics* 17, no. 4 (2008): 306–319; Atif Mian, Amir Sufi, and Francesco Trebbi, "Foreclosures, House Prices, and the Real Economy," *Journal of Finance* 70, no. 6 (2015): 2587–2634.

2. Byron Lutz, Raven Molloy, and Hui Shan, "The Housing Crisis and State and Local Government Tax Revenue: Five Channels," *Regional Science and Urban Economics*, 41 (2011): 306–319.

3. Davin Reed and Eileen Divringi, *Household Rental Debt during COVID-19*. Federal Reserve Bank of Philadelphia report, October 2020, www.philadelphiafed .org/-/media/frbp/assets/community-development/reports/household-rental -debt-during-covid-19.pdf.

4. Joint Center for Housing Studies, *State of the Nation's Housing* (Harvard University, 2020).

5. Jenny Schuetz and Sarah Crump, "What the U.S. Can Learn from Rental Housing Markets across the Globe," Brookings Institution essay, April 20, 2021, www.brookings.edu/essay/intro-rental-housing-markets/.

6. Edward Glaeser and Joseph Gyourko, "Urban Decline and Durable Housing," *Journal of Political Economy* 113, no. 2 (2005): 345–375.

7. Raven Molloy, Christopher Smith, and Abigail Wozniak, "Job Changing and the Decline in Long-Distance Migration in the United States," *Demography* 54, no. 2 (2017): 631–653.

8. Raj Chetty et al., "Where Is the Land of Opportunity? The Geography of Inter-generational Mobility in the United States," *Quarterly Journal of Economics* 129, no. 4 (2014): 1553–1623; Raj Chetty, Nathaniel Hendren, and Lawrence Katz, "The Effects of Exposure to Better Neighborhoods on Children: New Evidence from the Moving to Opportunity Experiment," *American Economic Review* 106, no. 4 (2016): 855–902.

9. Adam Levitin and Susan Wachter, *The Great American Housing Bubble: What Went Wrong and How We Can Protect Ourselves in the Future* (Harvard University Press, 2020); Mehrsa Baradaran, *The Color of Money: Black Banks and the Racial Wealth Gap* (Belknap Press of Harvard University Press, 2017); Dan Immergluck, *Foreclosed: High-Risk Lending, Deregulation, and the Undermining of America's Mortgage Market* (Cornell University Press, 2011).

Chapter 2

1. Jan Brueckner, "The Structure of Urban Equilibria: A Unified Treatment of the Muth-Mills Model," *Handbook of Urban and Regional Economics* 2, no. 20 (1987): 821–845.

2. Genevieve Giuliano and Ajay Agarwal, "Land Use Impacts of Transportation Investments," in *The Geography of Urban Transportation*, 4th ed., Genevieve Giuliano and Susan Hanson (eds.) (New York: Guilford Press, 2017), 218–246.

3. Keith Ihlanfeldt, "The Deconcentration of Minority Students Attending Bad Schools: The Role of Housing Affordability within School Attendance Zones Containing Good Schools," *Journal of Housing Economics* 43 (2019): 83–101.

4. Wallace E. Oates, "The Effects of Property Taxes and Local Public Spending on Property Values: An Empirical Study of Tax Capitalization and the Tiebout Hypothesis," *Journal of Political Economy* 77, no. 6 (1969): 957–971; Patrick Bayer, Fernando Ferreira, and Robert McMillan, "A Unified Framework for Measuring Preferences for Schools and Neighborhoods," *Journal of Political Economy* 115, no. 4 (2007): 588–638.

5. Sarah Crump et al., *Zoned Out: Why Massachusetts Needs to Legalize Apartments Near Transit*, Boston Indicators report, 2020, www.bostonindicators.org/reports/report-website-pages/zoned-out.

6. Hannah Hoyt and Jenny Schuetz, *Making Apartments More Affordable Starts with Understanding the Costs of Building Them* (Harvard University Joint Center for Housing Studies, 2020).

7. Land value estimates are taken from the dataset created by Morris Davis,

William Larsen, Stephen Oliner, and Jessica Shui, "The Price of Residential Land for Counties, ZIP codes, and Census Tracts in the United States," (Federal Housing Finance Agency working paper, no. 19-01, 2021), www.fhfa.gov/PolicyPro gramsResearch/Research/Pages/wp1901.aspx.

8. Jenny Schuetz, *Is Zoning a Regulatory Barrier or a Useful Tool?* Brookings Institution report, October 31, 2019, www.brookings.edu/research/is-zoning-a -useful-tool-or-a-regulatory-barrier/.

9. Amy Dain, *The State of Zoning for Multifamily Housing in Greater Boston*, Housing Toolbox, June 2019, www.housingtoolbox.org/writable/files/resources /AMY-DAIN_Multi-Family_Housing_Report.pdf; Jenny Schuetz, "Guarding the Town Walls: Mechanisms and Motives for Restricting Multifamily Housing in Massachusetts," *Real Estate Economics* 36, no. 3 (2008): 555–586.

10. Noah Kazis, "Public Actors, Private Law: Local Governments' Use of Covenants to Regulate Land Use," *Yale Law Review* 124 (2014): 1790–1824.

11. Allison Schertzer, Tate Twinam, and Randall Walsh, "Zoning and Segregation in Urban Economic History," *Regional Science and Urban Economics* (forthcoming 2021).

12. Susan S. Fanstein and Norman I. Fanstein, "Local Control as Social Reform: Planning for Big Cities in the Seventies," *Journal of the American Institute of Planners* 42, no. 3 (1976): 275–285.

13. Katherine L. Einstein, David M. Glick, and Maxwell Palmer, *Neighborhood Defenders: Participatory Politics and America's Housing Crisis* (Cambridge University Press, 2019).

14. Emily Badger and Quoctrung Bui, "Cities Start to Question an American Ideal: A House with a Yard on Every Lot," *New York Times*, June 18, 2019, www.ny times.com/interactive/2019/06/18/upshot/cities-across-america-question-single -family-zoning.html.

15. Robert C. Ellickson, "The Zoning Strait-Jacket: The Freezing of American Neighborhoods of Single-Family Houses," Yale Law School Public Law Research Paper, 2020, https://dx.doi.org/10.2139/ssrn.3507803; Salim Furth and Matthew Nolan Gray, "Do Minimum-Lot-Size Regulations Limit Housing Supply in Texas?" George Mason University Mercatus Center research paper, 2019, www.mercatus .org/system/files/gray-minimum-lot-size-mercatus-research-v3.pdf; Desegregate CT, *Connecticut Zoning Atlas*, 2021, www.desegregatect.org/atlas.

16. Cecile Murray and Jenny Schuetz, Is *California's Housing Market Broken? The Relationship Between Zoning, Rents, and Multifamily Development*, UC Berkeley Terner Center for Housing Innovation report, 2019.

17. Conor Dougherty, *Golden Gates: Fighting for Housing in America* (New York: Penguin, 2020).

18. The White House, Fact Sheet: The American Jobs Plan, March 31, 2021, www.whitehouse.gov/briefing-room/statements-releases/2021/03/31/fact-sheet -the-american-jobs-plan/.

19. Schuetz, *Is Zoning a Useful Tool?*

20. Chang-Tai Hsieh and Enrico Moretti, "Housing Constraints and Spatial Misallocation," *American Economic Journal: Macroeconomics* 11, no. 2 (2019): 1–39; Joseph Gyourko and Raven Molloy, "Regulation and Housing Supply" (National Bureau of Economic Research working paper, 2014); Edward Glaeser and Joseph Gyourko, "The Economic Implications of Housing Supply," *Journal of Economic Perspectives* 32, no. 1 (2018): 3–30.

21. California in particular has several statewide laws that exacerbate tight zoning and housing affordability—notably the California Environmental Quality Act (CEQA) and property tax distortions created by the 1978 Proposition 13. Addressing these complex but state-specific issues could fill an entire book; Connor Dougherty's recent book, *Golden Gates*, is an excellent starting point.

22. Jenny Schuetz, "Teardowns, Popups, and Renovations: How Does Housing Supply Change?" *Journal of Regional Science* 60, no. 3 (2020): 459–480.

23. C. Tsuriel Somerville and Christopher Mayer, "Government Regulation and Changes to the Affordable Housing Stock," *FRBNY Economic Policy Review* 9, no. 2 (2003): 45–62.

24. Raj Chetty et al., "Where Is the Land of Opportunity? The Geography of Inter-generational Mobility in the United States," *Quarterly Journal of Economics* 129, no. 4 (2014): 1553–1623.

25. Raj Chetty, Nathaniel Hendren, and Lawrence Katz, "The Effects of Exposure to Better Neighborhoods on Children: New Evidence from the Moving to Opportunity Experiment," *American Economic Review* 106, no. 4 (2016): 855–902.

26. Jens Ludwig et al., "Long-Term Neighborhood Effects on Low-Income Families: Evidence from Moving to Opportunity," *American Economic Review* 103, no. 3 (2013): 226–231.

Chapter 3

1. U.S. Global Change Research Program, Impacts, Risks, and Adaptation in the United States: Fourth National Climate Assessment, Vol. 2. Washington, DC, 2018, https://nca2018.globalchange.gov/.

2. U.S. Census Bureau, American Community Survey 1-Year Estimates, 2019 [Table S0801]; Adie Tomer, "America's Commuting Choices: 5 Major Takeaways from 2016 Census Data," The Avenue (blog), Brookings Institution, October 3, 2017, www.brookings.edu/blog/the-avenue/2017/10/03/americans-commuting -choices-5-major-takeaways-from-2016-census-data/.

3. Christopher Jones and Daniel Kammen, "Spatial Distribution of U.S. Household Carbon Footprints Undermines Greenhouse Gas Benefits of Urban Population Density," *Environmental Science and Technology* 48 (2014): 895–902.

4. Joseph W. Kane, "Banning Cars Won't Solve America's Bigger Transportation Problem: Long Trips," *The Avenue* (blog), Brookings Institution, January 6, 2020, www.brookings.edu/blog/the-avenue/2020/01/06/banning-cars-wont -solve-americas-bigger-transportation-problem-long-trips/.

5. U.S. Department of Transportation, National Household Travel Survey. Federal Highway Administration data, 2017, https://nhts.ornl.gov/.

6. Sam Bass Warner, *Streetcar Suburbs: The Process of Growth in Boston, 1870– 1900* (Harvard University Press, 1978); Kenneth T. Jackson, *Crabgrass Frontier: The Suburbanization of the United States* (Oxford University Press, 1985).

7. Geoff Boeing, "Off the Grid . . . and Back Again? The Recent Evolution of American Street Network Planning and Design," *Journal of the American Planning Association* 87, no. 1 (2020): 123–137.

8. Hamid Iravani and Venkat Rao, "The Effects of New Urbanism on Public Health," *Journal of Urban Design* 25, no. 2 (2020): 218–235; Emily Talen and Julia Koschinsky, "Compact, Walkable, Diverse Neighborhoods: Assessing Effects on Residents," *Housing Policy Debate* 24, no. 4 (2014): 717–750.

9. Intergovernmental Panel on Climate Change, *Global Warming of 1.5°C*. IPCC Special Report (Geneva, Switzerland, 2018), www.ipcc.ch/sr15/.

10. Margaret Wall, Nicholas Magliocca, and Virginia McConnell, "Modeling Coastal Land and Housing Markets: Understanding the Competing Influences of Amenities and Storm Risks," *Ocean and Coastal Management* 157 (May 1, 2018): 95–110.

11. Stuart A. Thompson and Yaryna Serkez, "Every Place Has Its Own Climate Risk. What Is It Where You Live?" *New York Times*, September 18, 2020, www.ny times.com/interactive/2020/09/18/opinion/wildfire-hurricane-climate.html.

12. Jim Morrison, "Climate Change Turns the Tide on Waterfront Living," *Washington Post Magazine*, April 13, 2020, www.washingtonpost.com/magazine/ 2020/04/13/after-decades-waterfront-living-climate-change-is-forcing-communi ties-plan-their-retreat-coasts/.

13. Nadja Popovich and Winston Choi-Schagrin, "Hidden Toll of the Northwest Heat Wave: Hundreds of Extra Deaths," *New York Times*, August 11, 2021, www.nytimes.com/interactive/2021/08/11/climate/deaths-pacific-northwest -heat-wave.html.

14. Zach Wichter, "Too Hot to Fly? Climate Change May Take a Toll on Air Travel," *New York Times*, June 20, 2017, www.nytimes.com/2017/06/20/business/ flying-climate-change.html; Zachary Hansen, "Nope, Turns Out It Was Techni-

cally Never Too Hot to Fly Out of Phoenix," azcentral, July 24, 2018, www.azcentral
.com/story/news/local/phoenix-weather/2018/07/24/phoenix-flights-never-too
-hot-fly-out-sky-harbor-airport-american-airlines/827871002/.

15. Robert I. McDonald et al., "Water on an Urban Planet: Urbanization and
the Reach of Urban Water Infrastructure," *Global Environmental Change* 27 (2014):
96–105; Bonnie Berkowitz and Adrian Blanco, "Mapping the Strain on Our Water,"
Washington Post, 2019, www.washingtonpost.com/climate-environment/2019/08
/06/mapping-strain-our-water/.

16. Benjamin J. Keys and Philip Mulder, "Neglected No More: Housing Markets, Mortgage Lending, and Sea Level Rise" (National Bureau of Economic Research working paper, 2020); Kristina Dahl et al, *Underwater: Rising Seas, Chronic
Floods, and the Implications for US Coastal Real Estate*, Union of Concerned Scientists report, 2018, www.ucsusa.org/resources/underwater.

17. Keys and Mulder, "Neglected No More."

18. Kimberley Thomas et al., "Explaining Differential Vulnerability to Climate
Change: A Social Science Review," *WIREs Climate Change* 10, no. 2 (2018): 1–18.

19. National Oceanic and Atmospheric Administration, "Economics and Demographics," Office for Coastal Management Fast Facts, 2021, https://coast.noaa
.gov/states/fast-facts/economics-and-demographics.html.

20. Wall et al., "Modeling Coastal Land and Housing Markets."

21. Thomas et al. (2018) provide a thorough review of the extensive literature on
racial disparities in climate impacts across the United States and internationally.

22. Laura A. Bakkensen and Lala Ma, "Sorting Over Flood Risk and Implications for Policy Reform," *Journal of Environmental Economics and Management* 104
(2020): 1–22, https://doi.org/10.1016/j.jeem.2020.102362.

23. Stephen M. Strader and Walker S. Ashley, "Finescale Assessment of Mo-
bile-Home Tornado Vulnerability in the Central and Southeast U.S.," *Weather,
Climate and Society* 10, no. 4 (2018): 797–812, https://journals.ametsoc.org/view/
journals/wcas/10/4/wcas-d-18-0060_1.xml.

24. Brad Plumer and Nadja Popovich, "How Decades of Racist Housing Policy
Left Neighborhoods Sweltering," *New York Times*, August 24, 2020, www.nytimes
.com/interactive/2020/08/24/climate/racism-redlining-cities-global-warming
.html.

25. Richard Rothstein, *The Color of Law: A Forgotten History of How Our Gov-
ernment Segregated America* (New York: Liveright Publishing, 2017); Jessica
Trounstine, *Segregation by Design: Local Politics and Inequality in American Cities*
(Cambridge University Press, 2018).

26. Christopher Flavelle and Kalen Goodluck, "Dispossessed, Again: Climate

Change Hits Native Americans Especially Hard," *New York Times*, June 27, 2021, www.nytimes.com/2021/06/27/climate/climate-Native-Americans.html; Nancy Pindus et al., "Housing Needs of American Indians and Alaska Natives in Tribal Areas," U.S. Department of Housing and Urban Development, Office of Policy Development and Research, 2017.

27. Kimberley Thomas et al., "Explaining Differential Vulnerability."

28. Alberto Alesina and Eliana La Ferrara, "Who Trusts Others?" *Journal of Public Economics* 85, no. 2 (2002): 207–234.

29. Michalis Diakakis et al., "Hurricane Sandy Mortality in the Caribbean and Continental North America," *Disaster Prevention and Management* 24, no. 1 (2015): 132–148.

30. Adrian Florido, "Two Years After Hurricane Maria Hit Puerto Rico, The Exact Death Toll Remains Unknown," NPR, *All Things Considered*, September 4, 2019, www.npr.org/2019/09/24/763958799/2-years-after-hurricane-maria-hit -puerto-rico-the-exact-death-toll-remains-unkno; Nishant Kishore et al., "Mortality in Puerto Rico after Hurricane Maria," *New England Journal of Medicine* 379, no. 2 (2018): 162–170; Elizabeth L. Andrade et al., "Mortality Reporting and Rumor Generation: An Assessment of Crisis and Emergency Risk Communication following Hurricane María in Puerto Rico," *Journal of Crisis and Risk Communication Research* 3, no. 1 (2020): 15–48.

31. Eric Klinenberg, "Denaturalizing Disaster: A Social Autopsy of the 1995 Chicago Heat Wave," *Theory and Society* 28, no. 2 (1999): 239–295.

32. Ryan Sabalow, Phillip Reese, and Dale Kasler, "These California Communities Could Be the Next Paradise. Is Yours One of Them?" *Sacramento Bee*, April 29, 2019, www.sacbee.com/news/california/fires/article227589484.html.

33. Richard Rothstein, *The Color of Law*; Kriston Capps and Christopher Cannon, "Redlined, Now Flooding," Bloomberg CityLab, March 15, 2021, www .bloomberg.com/graphics/2021-flood-risk-redlining/.

34. The Urban Institute's chartbook provides current estimates of mortgage originations and securitizations for conforming loans (excluding high-value "jumbo" loans). www.urban.org/sites/default/files/publication/102088/april -chartbook-2020.pdf.

35. Federal Housing Finance Agency, Fannie Mae and Freddie Mac, www.fhfa .gov/SupervisionRegulation/FannieMaeandFreddieMac.

36. Two other federal agencies, the Federal Housing Administration and the Veterans Administration, also originate or guarantee mortgage loans. Their combined market share is about half of the two GSEs. Very large mortgages, called jumbo loans, are securitized by private companies.

37. Amine Ouazad and Matthew Kahn, "Mortgage Finance and Climate Change: Securitization Dynamics in the Aftermath of Natural Disasters" (National Bureau of Economic Research working paper, 2021); Keys and Mulder, "Neglected No More."

38. Robert E. Litan and John Fleming, *The Climate Wolf at the Door: Why and How Climate Resilience Should Be Central to Building Back Better*, Brookings Institution report, 2021.

39. Christopher Flavelle and Emily Cochrane, "Chuck Schumer Stalls Climate Overhaul of Flood Insurance Program," *New York Times*, March 18, 2021, www.ny times.com/2021/03/18/climate/chuck-schumer-fema-flood-insurance.html.

40. Federal Emergency Management Agency, "Most Homeowners Insurance Does Not Cover Flooding," 2020, www.fema.gov/sites/default/files/2020-05/F061 _Homeowners_Does_not_cover_flooding.pdf.

41. Audie Cornish, interview with Glenn Pomeroy, NPR, *All Things Considered*, podcast audio, July 9, 2019.

42. Carolyn Kousky, "Financing Flood Losses: A Discussion of the National Flood Insurance Program," Resources for the Future, Discussion Paper 17-03, February 2017, https://media.rff.org/documents/RFF-DP-17-03.pdf.

43. Jonathan Spader and Jennifer Turnham, "CDBG Disaster Recovery Assistance and Homeowners' Rebuilding Outcomes Following Hurricanes Katrina and Rita," *Housing Policy Debate* 24, no. 1 (2014): 213–237; GAO, "Federal Assistance for Permanent Housing Primarily Benefited Homeowners; Opportunities Exist to Better Target Rental Needs" (Washington, DC: GAO-10-17, 2010); GAO, "Disaster Recovery: Better Monitoring of Block Grant Funds Is Needed" (Washington, DC: GAO-19-232, 2019).

44. Cristina E. Muñoz and Eric Tate, "Unequal Recovery? Federal Resource Distribution after a Midwest Flood Disaster," *International Journal of Environmental Research and Public Health* 13, no. 5 (2016): 507.

45. Kris Bertelson, "Renters and Homeowners Insurance: When the Unexpected Happens," Federal Reserve Bank of Saint Louis, Page One Economics, 2020, https://research.stlouisfed.org/publications/page1-econ/2020/02/03/renters-and -homeowners-insurance-when-the-unexpected-happens.

46. An enormous academic literature has investigated and debated the causes of suburbanization. Kenneth Jackson's *Crabgrass Frontier* presents a long-term historical take. Mieskowski and Mills (1993) summarize the economic literature through the early 1990s. Baum-Snow (2007) and Brinckman and Lin (2019) focus on the role of federally funded highways in encouraging decentralization. Kenneth Jackson, *Crabgrass Frontier: The Suburbanization of the United States* (Oxford University Press, 1987); Peter Mieszkowski and Edwin S. Mills, "The Causes of

Metropolitan Suburbanization," *Journal of Economic Perspectives* 7, no. 3 (1993): 135–147; Nathaniel Baum-Snow, "Did Highways Cause Suburbanization?" *Quarterly Journal of Economics* 122, no. 2 (2007): 775–805; and Jeffrey Brinkman and Jeffrey Lin, "Freeway Revolts!" (Federal Reserve Bank of Philadelphia, working paper, no. 19-29), www.philadelphiafed.org/-/media/frbp/assets/working-papers/2019/wp19-29.pdf.

47. Richard Rothstein, *The Color of Law*; Jessica Trounstine, *Segregation by Design*.

48. Congressional Budget Office, "Highway Trust Fund Accounts—CBO's January 2019 Baseline," January 2019, www.cbo.gov/system/files/2019-01/51300-2019-01-highwaytrustfund.pdf.

49. Ellen Dunham-Jones and June Williamson, *Retrofitting Suburbia* (Hoboken, NJ: John Wiley & Sons, 2008).

50. Mosaic District, Fairfax, VA, www.fxva.com/listing/mosaic/2326/; Spectrum Center, Irvine, CA, www.irvinespectrumcenter.com/.

51. Jaclene Begley and Lauren Lambie-Hanson, "The Home Maintenance and Improvement Behaviors of Older Adults in Boston," *Housing Policy Debate* 25, no. 4 (2015): 754–781.

52. U.S. Department of Energy, www.energy.gov/eere/wap/weatherization-assistance-program.

Chapter 4

1. Jonathan Gruber, *Public Finance and Public Policy*, 6th ed. (New York: MacMillan, 2019).

2. Center on Budget and Policy Priorities, "Policy Basics: Federal Rental Assistance," updated November 15, 2017, www.cbpp.org/research/housing/federal-rental-assistance.

3. Alan Mallach, "Rents Will Only Go So Low No Matter How Much We Build," Shelterforce, December 13, 2019, https://shelterforce.org/2019/12/13/rents-will-only-go-so-low-no-matter-how-much-we-build/.

4. U.S. Department of Housing and Urban Development, "Rental Burdens: Rethinking Affordability Measures," *PD&R Edge Magazine*, 2014, www.huduser.gov/portal/pdredge/pdr_edge_featd_article_092214.html.

5. Jeff Larrimore and Jenny Schuetz, "Assessing the Severity of Rent Burden on Low Income Families," Board of Governors of the Federal Reserve System FEDS Note, 2017; Jenny Schuetz, *Cost, Crowding, or Commuting? Housing Stresses on the Middle Class*, Brookings Institution report, May 7, 2019, www.brookings.edu/research/cost-crowding-or-commuting-housing-stress-on-the-middle-class/.

6. Martha Ross, Nicole Bateman, and Alec Friedhoff, "Meet the Low-Wage

Workforce," Brookings Institution interactive, March 2020, www.brookings.edu/
interactives/low-wage-workforce/.

7. Matthew Desmond, *Evicted: Poverty and Profit in the American City* (New
York: Crown, 2016); Kathryn J. Edin and H. Luke Shaffer, *$2.00 a Day: Living on
Almost Nothing in America* (New York: Houghton Mifflin Harcourt, 2016).

8. Lei Ding, Jackelyn Hwang, and Eileen Divringi, "Gentrification and Residential Mobility in Philadelphia," *Regional Science and Urban Economics* 61 (2016):
38–51.

9. Schuetz, *Cost, Crowding, or Commuting?*

10. Conor Dougherty, *Golden Gates: Fighting for Housing in America* (New York:
Penguin, 2020).

11. Claudia D. Solari and Robert D. Mare, "Housing Crowding Effects on Children's Wellbeing," *Social Science Research* 41, no. 2 (2012): 464–476.

12. Mark Mather, Dan A. Black, and Seth G. Sanders, *Standards of Living in
Appalachia: 1960 to 2000*, Population Reference Bureau report, 2007, www.prb.org
/livingstandardsappalachia/; Appalachian Regional Commission, *Appalachia: A
Report by the President's Appalachian Regional Commission, 1964* (U.S. Government Printing Office, 1964).

13. Nancy Pindus et al., *Housing Needs of American Indians and Alaska Natives
in Tribal Areas* (U.S. Department of Housing and Urban Development, Office of
Policy Development and Research, 2017); Desi Rodriguez-Lonebear et al., "American Indian Reservations and COVID-19: Correlates of Early Infection Rates in
the Pandemic," *Journal of Public Health Management & Practice* 26, no. 4 (2020):
371–377.

14. Eileen Divringi et al., *Measuring and Understanding Home Repair Costs:
A National Typology of Households*, Federal Reserve Bank of Philadelphia report,
2019; Jaclene Begley and Lauren Lambie-Hanson, "The Home Maintenance and
Improvement Behaviors of Older Adults in Boston," *Housing Policy Debate* 25, no.
4 (2015): 754–781.

15. Sarah Moon, Eliott C. McLaughlin, and Phil Gast, "Man Acquitted of 36
Deaths in Oakland's Ghost Ship fire; Hung Jury on Other Defendant," CNN, September 5, 2019, www.cnn.com/2019/09/05/us/ghost-ship-fire-oakland-verdict/
index.html; Peter Jamison and Peter Hermann, "'A Failing of the Systems': In Rowhouse Fire, D.C. Missed Many Chances to Save Lives," *Washington Post*, September
14, 2019, www.washingtonpost.com/local/dc-politics/a-failing-of-the-systems
-in-rowhouse-fire-dc-missed-many-chances-to-save-lives/2019/09/14/78536312
-d4bd-11e9-86ac-0f250cc91758_story.html; Jake Wegman, "Informal Housing in
the United States," *International Journal of Urban and Regional Research* 41, no. 2
(2017): 282–297.

16. U.S. Department of Housing and Urban Development, "Point-in-Time Count and Housing Inventory Count," 2017, www.hudexchange.info/programs /hdx/pit-hic/; Sharon McDonald, "The 2019 Point-in-Time Count: What Did We Learn about Family Homelessness?" *Children and Families* (blog), National Alliance to End Homelessness, 2020, https://endhomelessness.org/the-2019-point-in -time-count-what-did-we-learn-about-family-homelessness/.

17. U.S. Department of Housing and Urban Development, *HUD 2020 Continuum of Care Homeless Assistance Programs Homeless Populations and Sub-populations*, https://files.hudexchange.info/reports/published/CoC_PopSub_ NatlTerrDC_2020.pdf.

18. U.S. Department of Housing and Urban Development, *Worst Case Housing Needs 2019 Report to Congress*, 2020, www.huduser.gov/portal/publications/worst -case-housing-needs-2020.html.

19. Eileen Divringi et al., *Measuring and Understanding Home Repair Costs: A National Typology of Households*, Federal Reserve Bank of Philadelphia report, 2019.

20. Jenny Schuetz, "Housing Affordability and Quality Create Stress for Heartland Families," *The Avenue* (blog), Brookings Institution, July 2, 2019, www .brookings.edu/blog/the-avenue/2019/07/02/housing-affordability-and-quality -create-stress-for-heartland-families/.

21. Franklin D. Roosevelt, One Third of a Nation, second inaugural address, January 20, 1937, http://historymatters.gmu.edu/d/5105/.

22. *WHO Housing and Health Guidelines. Household Crowding* (Geneva: World Health Organization, 2018), www.ncbi.nlm.nih.gov/books/NBK535289/; Noa Pinter-Wollman, Andrea Jelić, and Nancy M. Wells, "The Impact of the Built Environment on Health Behaviors and Disease Transmission in Social Systems," *Philosophical Transactions of the Royal Society* B 373, no. 1753 (2018): 1–18, https:// doi.org/10.1098/rstb.2017.0245.

23. Furman Center for Real Estate and Urban Policy, "COVID-19 Cases in New York City, a Neighborhood-Level Analysis," *The Stoop* (blog), Furman Center for Real Estate and Urban Policy, 2020, https://furmancenter.org/thestoop/entry/ covid-19-cases-in-new-york-city-a-neighborhood-level-analysis; Jackie Botts and Lo Benichou, *The Neighborhoods Where COVID Collides with Overcrowded Homes*, Cal Matters report, 2020, https://calmatters.org/projects/california-coronavirus -overcrowded-neighborhoods-homes/.

24. Matthew Goldstein, "How Does the Federal Eviction Moratorium Work? It Depends Where You Live," *New York Times*, September 2, 2020, www.nytimes .com/2020/09/02/us/elections/the-cdc-has-ordered-a-moratorium-on-evictions -for-most-renters.html.

25. Tama Leventhal and Sandra Newman, "Housing and Child Development,"

Children and Youth Services Review 32, no. 9 (2010): 1165–1174; Carla Campbell et al., "A Case Study of Environmental Injustice: The Failure in Flint," *International Journal of Environmental Research and Public Health* 13, no. 10 (2016): 951.

26. Solari and Mare, "Housing Crowding Effects."

27. Center on Budget and Policy Priorities, "Policy Basics: The Earned Income Tax Credit," 2019, www.cbpp.org/research/federal-tax/the-earned-income-tax -credit.

28. Hilary Hoynes and Ankur J. Patel, "Effective Policy for Reducing Poverty and Inequality? The Earned Income Tax Credit and the Distribution of Income," *Journal of Human Resources* 53, no. 4 (2018): 859–890; Isabel Sawhill and Quentin Karpilow, *Raising the Minimum Wage and Redesigning the EITC*, Brookings Institution report, 2014, www.brookings.edu/research/raising-the-minimum-wage -and-redesigning-the-eitc/.

29. Center on Budget and Policy Priorities, "Policy Basics: The Child Tax Credit," 2019, www.cbpp.org/research/federal-tax/policy-basics-the-child-tax -credit.

30. Chuck Marr et al., "American Rescue Plan Includes Critical Expansions of Child Tax Credit and EITC," Center on Budget and Policy Priorities, March 12, 2021, www.cbpp.org/sites/default/files/3-12-21tax.pdf.

31. Desmond, *Evicted.*

32. Urban-Brookings Tax Policy Center, www.taxpolicycenter.org/taxvox/ how-fix-advanced-earned-income-tax-credit-lesson-health-reform.

33. U.S. Department of Labor, Minimum Wage, 2021, www.dol.gov/general/ topic/wages/minimumwage#:~:text=The%20federal%20minimum%20wage%20 for,of%20the%20two%20minimum%20wages.

34. Hilary Hoynes and Jesse Rothstein, "Universal Basic Income in the US and Advanced Countries" (NBER working paper, no. 25538, 2019).

35. Rachel Treisman, "California Program Giving $500 No-Strings-Attached Sipends Pays Off, Study Finds," NPR, March 4, 2021, www.npr.org/2021/03/04/ 973653719/california-program-giving-500-no-strings-attached-stipends-pays -off-study-finds.

36. Michael Eriksen and Amanda Ross, "Housing Vouchers and the Price of Rental Housing," *American Economic Journal: Economic Policy* 7, no. 3 (2015): 154–176.

37. Wendy Gamber, *The Boarding House in Nineteenth-Century America* (Johns Hopkins University Press, 2007).

38. Ingrid Gould Ellen, *What Do We Know about Housing Choice Vouchers?* NYU Furman Center report, 2018, https://furmancenter.org/research/publication/ what-do-we-know-about-housing-choice-vouchers266; Michelle Wood, Jennifer

Turnham, and Gregory Mills, "Housing Affordability and Family Well-Being: Results from the Housing Voucher Evaluation," *Housing Policy Debate* 19, no. 2 (2010): 367–412.

39. Carolin Schmidt, "Strong Tenant Protections and Subsidies Support Germany's Majority-Renter Housing Market," Brookings Institution essay, April 20, 2021, www.brookings.edu/essay/germany-rental-housing-markets/; Arthur Acolin, "The Public Sector Plays an Important Role in Supporting French Renters," Brookings Institution essay, April 20, 2021, www.brookings.edu/essay/france -rental-housing-markets/.

40. Eva Rosen, *The Voucher Promise: Section 8 and the Fate of an American Neighborhood* (Princeton University Press, 2020).

41. Peter Bergman et al., "Creating Moves to Opportunity: Experimental Evidence on Barriers to Neighborhood Choice" (National Bureau of Economic Research working paper, no. 26164, 2020), www.nber.org/papers/w26164; Heather L. Schwartz, Kata Mihaly, and Breann Gala, "Encouraging Residential Moves to Opportunity Neighborhoods: An Experiment Testing Incentives Offered to Housing Voucher Recipients," *Housing Policy Debate* 27, no. 2 (2017): 230–260.

42. Robert Collinson and Peter Ganong, "How Do Changes In Housing Voucher Design Affect Rent and Neighborhood Quality?" *American Economic Journal: American Economic Policy* 10, no. 2 (2018): 62–89, www.aeaweb.org/articles?id=10 .1257/pol.20150176.

43. Claudia Sahm, *Direct Stimulus Payments to Individuals*, Brookings Institution report, May 16, 2019, www.brookings.edu/research/direct-stimulus-pay ments-to-individuals.

44. Alex Schwartz, *Housing Policy in the United States*, 4th ed. (Abingdon: Taylor & Francis Group, 2006).

45. Jeff Andrews, "Affordable Housing Is in Crisis. Is Public Housing the Solution?" Curbed, January 13, 2020, www.curbed.com/2020/1/13/21026108/public -housing-faircloth-amendment-election-2020.

46. Carolina Reid, Adrian Napolitano, and Beatriz Stambuk-Torres, "The Costs of Affordable Housing Production: Insights from California's 9% Low-Income Housing Tax Credit Program," UC Berkeley Terner Center for Housing Innovation, 2020.

47. Ana Stefancic and Sam Tsemberis, "Housing First for Long-Term Shelter Dwellers with Psychiatric Disabilities in a Suburban County: A Four-Year Study of Housing Access and Retention," *Journal of Primary Prevention* 28 (2007): 265–279.

48. Jenny Schuetz, "Affordable Assisted Living: Surveying the Possibilities," Harvard University Joint Center for Housing Studies, 2003.

49. Arthur Acolin, "The Public Sector Plays an Important Role."

50. Tien-Foo Sing, I-Chun Tsai, and Ming-Chi Chen, "Price Dynamics in Public and Private Housing Markets in Singapore," *Journal of Housing Economics* 15 (2006): 305–320.

51. Christoph Reinprecht, "Social Housing in Austria," in *Social Housing in Europe*, Christine Whitehead and Kath Scanlon (eds.) (London School of Economics, 2007), 35–43.

52. Matthew Desmond, *Evicted* (Princeton University Press, 2017).

53. Meredith Greif, "Regulating Landlords: Unintended Consequences for Poor Tenants," *City and Community* 17, no. 3 (2018): 658–674.

54. Jenny Schuetz and Sarah Crump, "What the U.S. Can Learn from Rental Housing Markets around the Globe," Brookings Institution essay, April 20, 2021, www.brookings.edu/essay/intro-rental-housing-markets/.

Chapter 5

1. William G. Gale, Jonathan Gruber, and Seth Stephens-Davidowitz, "Encouraging Homeownership through the Tax Code," *Tax Notes* 115, no. 12 (June 1, 2007): 1171–1189.

2. William G. Gale, "It's Time to Gut the Mortgage Interest Deduction," *Up Front* (blog), Brookings Institution, November 6, 2017, www.brookings.edu/blog/up-front/2017/11/06/its-time-to-gut-the-mortgage-interest-deduction/; Dwight Jaffee and John Quigley, "The Future of the Government-Sponsored Enterprises: The Role for Government in the U.S. Mortgage Market," in *Housing and the Financial Crisis*, eds. Edward Glaeser and Todd Sinai (University of Chicago Press, 2013), 361–418.

3. "Let FHA Loans Help You," U.S. Department of Housing and Urban Development, www.hud.gov/buying/loans; Stuart W. Passmore and Alexander von Hafften, "Improving the 30-Year Fixed-Rate Mortgage" (FEDS working paper, no. 2017-090, August 25, 2017).

4. Richard H. Thaler and Shlomo Benartzi, "Save More Tomorrow™: Using Behavioral Economics to Increase Employee Saving," *Journal of Political Economy* 112, no. s1 (February 2004): 164–187.

5. Robert Lerman and Beno Braga. "Are Median Incomes Actually Stagnating? How We Calculate Housing Costs Affects the Answer," *Urban Wire* (blog), Urban Institute, November 6, 2018, www.urban.org/urban-wire/are-median-incomes-actually-stagnating-how-we-calculate-housing-costs-affects-answer.

6. Brent Ambrose and Sunwoong Kim, "Modeling the Korean Chonsei Lease Contract," *Real Estate Economics* 31, no. 1 (2003): 53–74; Jenny Schuetz, "Renting the American Dream: Why Homeownership Shouldn't Be a Prerequisite for Mid-

dle-Class Financial Security," *Up Front* (blog), Brookings Institution, February 13, 2019, www.brookings.edu/blog/up-front/2019/02/13/renting-the-american-dream-why-homeownership-shouldnt-be-a-pre-requisite-for-middle-class-financial-security/.

7. U.S. Securities and Exchange Commission, "Saving and Investing: A Roadmap to Your Financial Security through Saving and Investing," www.sec.gov/investor/pubs/sec-guide-to-savings-and-investing.pdf.

8. Home values taken from 1980 Decennial Census and 2018 ACS, adjusted for inflation.

9. "What Is the Average Time to Sell a House?" Zillow, October 2020, www.zillow.com/sellers-guide/average-time-to-sell-a-house/.

10. Julian Kheel, "How and When to Consider a 'Cash Out' Refinance," CNN, August 10, 2020, www.cnn.com/2020/08/10/cnn-underscored/cash-out-refinance-pros-and-cons/index.html; Ioannis Floros and Joshua T. White, "Qualified Residential Mortgages and Default Risk," *Journal of Banking and Finance* 70 (September 2016): 86–104.

11. Allison Schertzer, Tate Twinam, and Randall Walsh, "Zoning and Segregation in Urban Economic History," *Regional Science and Urban Economics* (forthcoming 2021).

12. Richard Rothstein, *The Color of Law: A Forgotten History of How Our Government Segregated America* (New York: Liveright Publishing, 2017).

13. Jeffrey Brinkman and Jeffrey Lin, "Freeway Revolts!" (Federal Reserve Bank of Philadelphia working paper, no. 19-29, 2019); Allison Shertzer, Tate Twinam, and Randall P. Walsh, "Race, Ethnicity, and Discriminatory Zoning," *American Economic Journal: Applied Economics* 8, no. 3 (July 2016): 217–246.

14. "Community Reinvestment Act," Federal Financial Institutions Examination Council, last modified October 9, 2020, www.ffiec.gov/cra/; Colleen Casey, Joseph Farhat, and Gregory Cartwright, "Community Reinvestment Act and Local Governance Contexts: Advancing the Future of Community Reinvestment?" *Cityscape: A Journal of Policy Development and Research* 19, no. 2 (2017): 137–160.

15. Andrew Hanson et al., "Discrimination in Mortgage Lending: Evidence from a Correspondence Experiment," *Journal of Urban Economics* 92 (2018): 48–65; Marsha Courchane and Stephen Ross, "Evidence and Actions on Mortgage Market Disparities: Research, Fair Lending Enforcement, and Consumer Protection," *Housing Policy Debate* 29, no. 5 (2019): 769–794.

16. Max Besbris and Jacob Faber, "Investigating the Relationship between Real Estate Agents, Segregation, and House Prices: Steering and Upselling in New York State," *Sociological Forum* 32, no. 4 (September 2017): 850–873; Elizabeth

Korver-Glenn, "Brokering Ties and Inequality: How White Real Estate Agents Recreate Advantage and Exclusion in Urban Housing Markets," *Social Currents* 5, no. 4 (2018): 350–368.

17. Miriam Jorgensen and Randall K. Q. Akee. "Access to Capital and Credit in Native Communities: A Data Review" (Tucson: Native Nations Institute, 2017).

18. Jacob Krimmel and Susan Wachter, "The Future of the Community Reinvestment Act" (Penn Institute for Urban Research working paper, 2019).

19. Darrick Hamilton and William Darrity Jr., "Can 'Baby Bonds' Eliminate the Racial Wealth Gap in a Putative Post-Racial America?" *Review of Black Political Economy* 37 (2010): 207–216.

20. Maury Gittleman and Edward N. Wolff, "Racial Differences in Patterns of Wealth Accumulation," *Journal of Human Resources* 39, no. 1 (2004): 193–227.

21. Neil Bhutta et al., "Disparities in Wealth by Race and Ethnicity in the 2019 Survey of Consumer Finances" (Board of Governors of the Federal Reserve: FEDS Notes, September 28, 2020).

22. Stuart A. Gabriel and Stuart S. Rosenthal, "Homeownership in the 1980s and 1990s: Aggregate Trends and Racial Gaps," *Journal of Urban Economics* 57, no. 1 (January 2005): 101–127.

23. Tom Mayock and Rachel Spritzer Malacrida, "Socioeconomic and Racial Disparities in the Financial Returns to Homeownership," *Regional Science and Urban Economics* 70 (May 2018): 80–96.

24. Debbie Gruenstein Bocian et al., "Foreclosures by Race and Ethnicity: The Demographics of a Crisis," Center for Responsible Lending report, June 18, 2010, www.mvfairhousing.com/ai2015/2010-06-18_Foreclosures_by_Race_and _Ethnicity.PDF; Carolina Reid et al., "Revisiting the Subprime Crisis: The Dual Mortgage Market and Mortgage Defaults by Race and Ethnicity," *Journal of Urban Affairs* 39, no. 4 (2017): 469–487.

25. Edward N. Wolff, "Household Wealth Trends in the United States, 1962 to 2016: Has Middle Class Wealth Recovered?" (National Bureau of Economic Research working paper, no. 24085, November 2017), www.nber.org/papers/w24085.

26. Michael J. Collins, Maximilian Schmeiser, and Carly Urban, "Protecting Minority Homeowners: Race, Foreclosure Counseling, and Mortgage Modifications," *Journal of Consumer Affairs* 47, no. 2 (2013): 289–310; Alanna McCargo, Jung Hyun Choi, and Edward Golding, "Building Black Homeownership Bridges: A Five-Point Framework for Reducing the Racial Homeownership Gap," Urban Institute, Housing Finance Policy Center, May 2019, www.urban.org/sites/default /files/publication/100204/building_black_ownership_bridges_1.pdf.

27. Denise DiPasquale and Edward Glaeser, "Incentives and Social Capital: Are Homeowners Better Citizens?" *Journal of Urban Economics* 45, no. 2 (1999):

354–384; Richard K. Green, Gary D. Painter, and Michelle J. White, *Measuring the Benefits of Homeowning: Effects on Children Redux*, Research Institute for Housing America special report, August 2012, http://citeseerx.ist.psu.edu/viewdoc/down load?doi=10.1.1.296.5702&rep=rep1&type=pdf; N. Edward Coulson and Hermann Li, "Measuring the External Benefits of Homeownership," *Journal of Urban Economics* 77 (2013): 57–67.

28. William A. Fischel, *The Homevoter Hypothesis: How Home Values Influence Local Government Taxation, School Finance, and Land-Use Policies* (Harvard University Press, 2001).

29. Jacqueline Rabe Thomas, "Separated by Design: How Some of America's Richest Towns Fight Affordable Housing," Connecticut Mirror with ProPublica, May 22, 2019, www.propublica.org/article/how-some-of-americas-richest-towns -fight-affordable-housing.

30. Katherine Levine Einstein, Maxwell Palmer, and David M. Glick, "Who Participates in Local Government? Evidence from Meeting Minutes," *Perspectives on Politics* 17, no. 1 (March 2019): 28–46.

31. Donald J. Trump, Twitter post, July 29, 2020, 12:19 p.m., https://twitter.com /realDonaldTrump/status/1288509568578777088.

32. Tax Policy Center, "Key Elements of the U.S. Tax System," Tax Policy Center Briefing Book, chapter 3, Urban Institute and Brookings Institution, 2021, www .taxpolicycenter.org/briefing-book.

33. Gale, Gruber, and Stephens-Davidowitz, "Encouraging Homeownership," 1171–1189; Andrew Hanson, "Size of Home, Homeownership, and the Mortgage Interest Deduction," *Journal of Housing Economics* 21, no. 3 (September 2012): 195–210; Christian A. L. Hilber and Tracy M. Turner, "The Mortgage Interest Deduction and Its Impact on Homeownership Decisions," *Review of Economics and Statistics* 96, no. 4 (October 2014): 618–637.

34. Howard Gleckman, "The TCJA Shifted the Benefits of Tax Expenditures to Higher-Income Households," Tax Policy Center: TaxVox, October 16, 2018, www.taxpolicycenter.org/taxvox/tcja-shifted-benefits-tax-expenditures-higher -income-households.

35. H. A. Morrow-Jones, "The Housing Life-Cycle and the Transition from Renting to Owning a Home in the United States: A Multistate Analysis," *Environment and Planning A: Economy and Space* 20, no. 9 (September 1988): 1165–1184; Jonathan Halket, "Saving Up or Settling Down: Home Ownership over the Life Cycle," *Review of Economic Dynamics* 17, no. 2 (April 2014): 345–366.

36. Jenny Schuetz and Sarah Crump. "What Can the U.S. Learn from Rental Housing Markets across the Globe?" Brookings Institution essay, April 20, 2021, https://www.brookings.edu/essay/intro-rental-housing-markets/.

37. Mark P. Keightley, "The Mortgage Interest Deduction," Congressional Research Service, In Focus, May 7, 2020, https://fas.org/sgp/crs/misc/IF11540.pdf.

38. Gale, Gruber, and Stephens-Davidowitz, "Encouraging Homeownership," 1171–1189. Advocates for the MID have argued that, because the tax benefits are capitalized into higher home values, eliminating the MID would lead to widespread house price depreciation. Early analysis of the TCJA shows no signs that reducing the cap from $1 million to $750,000 led to housing price declines, even in parts of the country where the policy was most salient. Further, the MID could be phased out gradually over a period of time.

39. There is a vast literature on how to increase U.S. households' participation in retirement savings programs, such as IRAs and 401(k) plans. Most of these programs penalize withdrawing funds before the household reaches retirement age. My focus in this chapter is on how households could accumulate savings that they can tap for current expenses or emergencies before retirement, I will not discuss the retirement savings literature.

40. John Beshears et al., "Building Emergency Savings through Employer-Sponsored Savings Accounts" (National Bureau of Economic Research working paper, no. 26498, November 2019).

41. Beshears et al. discuss considerations for self-employed workers or those whose employers do not offer 401(k) programs. A program could include federal matches for lower-income workers.

42. Neil Bhutta et al., "Disparities in Wealth."

43. Cory Booker, "Cory's Plan to Provide Safe, Affordable Housing for All Americans," June 2019, https://medium.com/@corybooker/corys-plan-to-provide -safe-affordable-housing-forall-americans-da1d83662baa.

44. Darrity and Hamilton, "Can 'Baby Bonds' Eliminate"; Darrity and Hamilton, "Bold Policies for Economic Justice," *The Review of Black Political Economy* 39, no. 1 (2012): 75–85.

45. Darrity and Hamilton, "Can 'Baby Bonds' Eliminate," 210.

46. Boshara, Ray, "Federal Policy and Asset Building" (Washington University in St. Louis, Center for Social Development working paper, no. 03-43, 2003); Margaret Sherraden et al., *Saving in Low Income Households: Evidence from Interviews with Participants in the American Dream Demonstration*, Washington University in St. Louis Center for Social Development report, 2005, https://openscholarship .wustl.edu/cgi/viewcontent.cgi?article=1339&context=csd_research.

47. Gregory Mills et al., "Effect of Individual Development Accounts on Asset Purchases and Saving Behavior: Evidence from a Controlled Experiment," *Journal of Public Economics* 92, no. 5–6 (2008): 1509–1530.

Chapter 6

1. Ray Oldenburg, *The Great Good Place. Cafes, Coffeeshops, Community Centers, Beauty Parlors, General Stores, Bars, Hangouts, and How They Get You through the Day* (St. Paul, MN: Paragon House, 1989).

2. Wallace E. Oates, "The Effects of Property Taxes and Local Public Spending on Property Values: An Empirical Study of Tax Capitalization and the Tiebout Hypothesis," *Journal of Political Economy* 77, no. 6 (1969): 957–971; Sung Hoon Kang, Mark Skidmore, and Laura Reese, "The Effects of Changes in Property Tax Rates and School Spending on Residential and Business Property Value Growth," *Real Estate Economics* 43, no. 2 (2015): 300–333; Paramita Dhar and Stephen L. Ross, "The Effects of Changes in Property Tax Rates and School Spending on Residential and Business Property Value Growth," *Journal of Urban Economics* 71, no. 1 (2012): 18–25; Phuong Nguyen-Hoang and John Yinger, "The Capitalization of School Quality into House Values: A Review," *Journal of Housing Economics* 20, no. 1 (2011): 30–48.

3. John McDonald and Daniel McMillen, "Reaction of House Prices to a New Rapid Transit Line: Chicago's Midway Line, 1983–1999," *Real Estate Economics* 32, no. 3 (2004): 463–486.

4. David S. Brookshire, "Valuing Public Goods: A Comparison of Survey and Hedonic Approaches," *American Economic Review* 72, no. 1 (1982): 165–177; Alan Williams, "The Optimal Provision of Public Goods in a System of Local Government," *Journal of Political Economy* 74, no. 1 (1966): 18–33.

5. Jenny Schuetz, *Who's to Blame for High Housing Costs? It's More Complicated Than You Think*, Brookings Institution report, January 17, 2020, www.brookings .edu/research/whos-to-blame-for-high-housing-costs-its-more-complicated -than-you-think/.

6. Hannah Hoyt and Jenny Schuetz, "Parking Requirements and Foundations Are Driving Up the Cost of Multifamily Housing," *Housing Perspectives* (blog), Harvard University Joint Center for Housing Studies, June 2, 2020, www.jchs.har vard.edu/blog/parking-requirements-and-foundations-are-driving-up-the-cost -of-multifamily-housing.

7. U.S. Census Bureau, "Characteristics of New Housing: Highlights," 2020, www.census.gov/construction/chars/highlights.html.

8. Richard F. Dye and Daniel P. McMillen, "Teardowns and Land Values in the Chicago Metropolitan Area," *Journal of Urban Economics* 61, no. 1 (2007): 45–63.

9. Eve Ewing, *Ghosts in the Schoolyard: Racism and School Closings on Chicago's South Side* (University of Chicago Press, 2018).

10. Justin Moyer and Julie Zauzmer, "A Record Rainfall This Month Left D.C.

Basements Flooded with Sewage: Financial Help Is on the Way," *Washington Post*, September 17, 2020, www.washingtonpost.com/local/dc-flooding-edgewood/2020/09/17/900bc6ce-f8e9-11ea-a510-f57d8ce76e11_story.html.

11. Ivan Penn, "Climate Change and Poor Planning Are Blamed for California Blackouts," *New York Times*, October 6, 2020, www.nytimes.com/2020/10/06/business/energy-environment/california-blackout-cause-report.html; Sammy Roth, "Texas Blackouts Show the Power Grid Isn't Ready for Climate Change," *Los Angeles Times*, February 16, 2021, www.latimes.com/environment/story/2021-02-16/texas-blackouts-california-climate-change.

12. James Alm, Robert Buschman, and David Sjoquist, "Rethinking Local Government Reliance on the Property Tax," *Regional Science and Urban Economics* 41, no. 4 (2011): 320–331; Nathan Anderson, "Property Tax Limitations: An Interpretive Review," *National Tax Journal* 59, no. 3 (2006): 685–694.

13. Lincoln Institute of Land Policy, "State-by-State Property Tax at a Glance," last updated 2020, www.lincolninst.edu/research-data/data-toolkits/significant-features-property-tax/state-state-property-tax-glance/property-tax-data-visualization.

14. Tracy Gordon, "Critics Argue the Property Tax Is Unfair. Do They Have a Point? Urban-Brookings Tax Policy Center, 2020, www.taxpolicycenter.org/taxvox/critics-argue-property-tax-unfair-do-they-have-point.

15. Joan Youngman, *A Good Tax* (Cambridge: Lincoln Institute of Land Policy, 2016).

16. Christopher Berry, "Reassessing the Property Tax" (University of Chicago working paper, 2021); Carlos Avenancio-Leon and Troup Howard, "The Assessment Gap: Racial Inequalities in Property Taxation" (Washington Center for Equitable Growth working paper, June 10, 2020).

17. District of Columbia Office of Tax and Revenue, "Homestead/Senior Citizen Deduction," 2020, https://otr.cfo.dc.gov/page/homesteadsenior-citizen-deduction.

18. Iris J. Lav and Michael Leachman, "State Limits on Property Taxes Hamstring Local Services and Should Be Relaxed or Repealed," July 18, 2018, www.cbpp.org/research/state-budget-and-tax/state-limits-on-property-taxes-hamstring-local-services-and-should-be#:~:text=Today%2C%2044%20states%20and%20the,as%20a%20local%20revenue%20source.

19. Nada Wasi and Michelle J. White, "Property Tax Limitations and Mobility: The Lock-in Effect of California's Proposition 13" (National Bureau of Economic Research working paper, no. 11108, 2005).

20. Legislative Analyst's Office, *Common Claims about Proposition 13*, LAO report, September 19, 2016, https://lao.ca.gov/Publications/Report/3497.

21. Liam Dillon and Ben Poston, "California Homeowners Get to Pass Property Taxes to Their Kids. It's Proved Highly Profitable to an Elite Group," *Los Angeles Times*, August 17, 2018, www.latimes.com/politics/la-pol-ca-california -property-taxes-elites-201808-htmlstory.html.

22. Mark Haveman and Terry Sexton, *Property Tax Assessment Limits: Lessons from 30 Years of Experience*, Lincoln Institute of Land Policy report (Cambridge, MA, 2008), www.lincolninst.edu/sites/default/files/pubfiles/property-tax -assessment-limits-full_0.pdf.

23. Louise Sheiner and Sophia Campbell, "How Much Is COVID-19 Hurting State and Local Revenues?" *Up Front* (blog), Brookings Institution, September 24, 2020, www.brookings.edu/blog/up-front/2020/09/24/how-much-is-covid-19 -hurting-state-and-local-revenues/; Sarah Crump and Jenny Schuetz, *What the Great Recession Can Teach Us about the Post-pandemic Housing Market*, Brookings Institution report, March 29, 2021, www.brookings.edu/research/what-the-great -recession-can-teach-us-about-the-post-pandemic-housing-market/.

24. Janelle Cammenga, "State and Local Sales Tax Rates," 2020, https:// taxfoundation.org/2020-sales-taxes/.

25. Tax Policy Center, "Briefing Book: The State of State (and Local) Tax Policy," Urban-Brookings Tax Policy Center, updated May 2020, www.taxpolicycenter .org/briefing-book/how-do-state-and-local-sales-taxes-work#:~:text=Forty -five%20states%20and%20the%20District%20of%20Columbia%20levy,allow% 20general%20sales%20taxes%20at%20the%20local%20level.

26. Jared Walczak, "Local Income Taxes in 2019," Tax Foundation, July 30, 2019, https://taxfoundation.org/local-income-taxes-2019/.

27. City of Philadelphia, "Payments, Assistance and Taxes," 2021, www.phila .gov/services/payments-assistance-taxes/business-taxes/wage-tax-employers/.

28. Vicki Been, "Impact Fees and Housing Affordability," *Cityscape: A Journal of Policy Development and Research* 8, no. 1 (2005): 139–185.

29. Kenneth Jackson. *Crabgrass Frontier: The Suburbanization of the United States* (Oxford University Press, 1985).

30. Jan Brueckner, "Infrastructure Financing and Urban Development: The Economics of Impact Fees," *Journal of Public Economics* 66, no. 3 (1997): 383–407.

31. Vicki Been, "Impact Fees and Housing Affordability," *Cityscape* 8, no. 1 (2005): 139–185.

32. Nollan v. California Coastal Commission, 483 U.S. 825 (1987); Dolan v. City of Tigard, 512 U.S. 374 (1994).

33. Jenny Schuetz, Rachel Meltzer, and Vicki Been, "31 Flavors of Inclusionary Zoning: Comparing Policies from San Francisco, Washington, DC, and Suburban Boston," *Journal of the American Planning Association* 75, no. 4 (2009): 441–456;

Lance Freeman and Jenny Schuetz, "Producing Affordable Housing in Rising Markets," *Cityscape* 19, no. 1 (2017): 217–236.

34. Alan Altshuler and Jose Antonio Gomez-Ibanez, *Regulation for Revenue: The Political Economy of Land Use Exactions* (Brookings Institution, 1993).

35. Brueckner, "Infrastructure Financing"; Jan Brueckner and Robert Helsley, "Sprawl and Blight," *Journal of Urban Economics* 69, no. 2 (2011): 205–213.

36. John Landis et al., *Pay to Play: Residential Development Fees in California Cities and Counties, 1999,*" State of California Department of Housing and Community Development report, August 2001, www.hcd.ca.gov/policy-research/plans-reports/docs/pay-to-play-fee-residential-development-fees-1999.pdf.

37. Hayley Raetz, David Garcia, and Nathanial Decker, *Residential Impact Fees in California*, UC-Berkeley Terner Center for Housing Innovation report, 2019; Gregory Burge and Keith Ihlanfeldt, "Impact Fees and Single-Family Home Construction," *Journal of Urban Economics* 60, no. 2 (2006): 284–306.

38. William A. Fischel, "Zoning and the Exercise of Monopoly Power: A Reevaluation," *Journal of Urban Economics* 8, no. 3 (1980): 283–293; William A. Fischel, "Fiscal Zoning and Economists' Views of the Property Tax" (Lincoln Institute of Land Policy working paper, 2013), www.lincolninst.edu/sites/default/files/pub files/2355_1695_Fischel_WP14WF1.pdf.

39. Leah Brooks and Zachary D. Liscow, "Infrastructure Costs," 2019, last revised March 20, 2020, https://dx.doi.org/10.2139/ssrn.3428675.

40. The concept of a land value tax was introduced by Henry George in his 1882 book, *Progress and Poverty*. While pure land taxes are scarce, a "split rate" property tax in which structures are taxed at a lower rate than land has some precedent among U.S. communities.

41. Jenny Schuetz, "To Improve Housing Affordability, We Need Better Alignment of Zoning, Taxes, and Subsidies," Brookings Institution, Policy 2020, Big Ideas, January 7, 2020, www.brookings.edu/policy2020/bigideas/to-improve-housing-af fordability-we-need-better-alignment-of-zoning-taxes-and-subsidies/.

42. Yonah Freemark, "Upzoning Chicago: Impacts of a Zoning Reform on Property Values and Housing Construction," *Urban Affairs Review* 56, no. 3 (2019): 758–759.

43. Joshua Vincent, "Neighborhood Revitalization and New Life: A Land Value Taxation Approach," *American Journal of Economics and Sociology* 71, no. 4 (2012): 1073–1094; Mark Alan Hughes, "Why So Little Georgism in America?" (Lincoln Institute for Land Policy working paper, 2006), www.lincolninst.edu/sites/default /files/pubfiles/1275_hughes_final.pdf.

44. Aravind Boddupalli and Erin Huffer, "What Do Federal Taxes Have To

Do with Your Public Transit?" Tax Policy Center, Urban Institute and Brookings Institution, March 2, 2020, www.taxpolicycenter.org/taxvox/what-do-federal -taxes-have-do-your-public-transit; Adie Tomer, "A Real Win for Metropolitan Areas in 2017 Transportation Budget," *The Avenue* (blog), Brookings Institution, February 22, 2016, www.brookings.edu/blog/the-avenue/2016/02/22/a-real-win -for-metropolitan-areas-in-2017-transportation-budget/.

45. U.S. Department of Housing and Urban Development, "Community Development Block Grant," www.hud.gov/program_offices/comm_planning/cdbg.

46. Barbara Biasi, "School Finance Equalization Increases Intergenerational Mobility: Evidence from a Simulated-Instruments Approach" (National Bureau of Economic Research working paper, no. 25600, 2019); Caroline M. Hoxby, "All School Finance Equalizations Are Not Created Equal," *Quarterly Journal of Economics* 116, no. 4 (2001): 1189–1231; William Fischel, "Did Serrano Cause Proposition 13?" *National Tax Journal* 42, no. 4 (1989): 465–473.

47. Matt Chingos and Kristin Blagg, "Do Poor Kids Get Their Fair Share of School Funding?" Urban Institute report, 2017, www.urban.org/sites/default/files /publication/90586/school_funding_brief_1.pdf.

48. Caroline M. Hoxby and Ilyana Kuziemko, "Robin Hood and His Not-So-Merry Plan: Capitalization and the Self-Destruction of Texas' School Finance Equalization Plan" (National Bureau of Economic Research working paper, no. 10722, 2004).

49. Jake Krimmel, "Reclaiming Local Control: School Finance Reforms and Housing Supply Restrictions" (working paper, July 28, 2021), https://static1.square space.com/static/5f75531c54380e4fb4b0f839/t/6101dc4b478e4578d6ff67bf/ 1627511883725/Krimmel_HousingSupply_SchoolFinance_draft_mostrecent .pdf.

50. Jan Brueckner and Robert Helsley, "Sprawl and Blight," *Journal of Urban Economics* 69, no. 2 (2011): 205–213.

Chapter 7

1. Richard D. Kahlenburg, "Taking on Class and Racial Discrimination in Housing," The American Prospect, August 2, 2018, https://prospect.org/civil -rights/taking-class-racial-discrimination-housing/.

2. Jenny Schuetz, *HUD Can't Fix Exclusionary Zoning by Withholding CDBG Funds*, Brookings Institution report, October 15, 2018, www.brookings.edu/re search/hud-cant-fix-exclusionary-zoning-by-withholding-cdbg-funds/.

3. Anika Singh Lemar, "The Role of States in Liberalizing Land Use Regulations," *North Carolina Law Review* 97 (2018): 293–354.

4. Liam Dillon, "A Key Reform of California's Environmental Law Hasn't Kept Its Promises," *Los Angeles Times*, January 24, 2017, www.latimes.com/politics/la -pol-sac-environmental-law-reform-failures-20170124-story.html.

5. Political scientists have created various categories for local government activities: redistributive, allocational, and developmental. Zoltan L. Hajnal and Jessica Trounstine, "Who or What Governs? The Effects of Economics, Politics, Institutions, and Needs on Local Spending," *American Politics Research* 38, no. 6 (2010): 1130–1163. Most housing-specific activities do not fall neatly into these categories. For instance, although localities administer subsidies to low-income households, the funding for these is mostly federal, so local leaders are not making decisions about redistribution among their constituents.

6. Beth Walter Honadle, "Theoretical and Practical Issues of Local Government Capacity in an Era of Devloution," *Journal of Regional Analysis and Policy* 31, no. 1 (2001): 77–90.

7. Charles Tiebout, "A Pure Theory of Public Expenditures," *Journal of Political Economy* 64, no. 5 (1956): 416–424.

8. U.S. Census Bureau American Community Survey, Demographic and Housing Estimates, Table DP05 (2019).

9. Wallace E. Oates, "The Effects of Property Taxes and Local Public Spending on Property Values: An Empirical Study of Tax Capitalization and the Tiebout Hypothesis," *Journal of Political Economy* 77, no. 6 (1969): 957–971; H. Spencer Banzhaf and Randall P. Walsh, "Segregation and Tiebout Sorting: Investigating the Link between Investments in Public Goods and Neighborhood Tipping" (National Bureau of Economic Research working paper, no. 16057, 2010); Patrick Bayer and Robert McMillan, "Tiebout Sorting and Neighborhood Stratification," *Journal of Public Economics* 96, no. 11 (2012): 1129–1143.

10. Elinor Ostrom, "Metropolitan Reform: Propositions Derived from Two Traditions," *Social Science Quarterly* 53, no. 3 (1972): 474–493.

11. Thomas M. Holbrook and Aaron C. Weinschenk, "Campaigns, Mobilization, and Turnout in Mayoral Elections," *Political Research Quarterly* 67, no. 1 (2013): 42–55.

12. Sidney Verba, Kay Lehman Schlozman, and Henry E. Brady, *Voice and Equality: Civic Volunteerism in American Politics* (Harvard University Press, 1995).

13. Verba, Schlozman, and Brody, *Voice and Equality*.

14. Katherine Einstein, Joseph Ornstein, and Maxwell Palmer, "Who Represents the Renters?" (working paper, 2021), http://chriswarshaw.com/lpe_ conference/EinsteinOrnsteinPalmer_Homeowners.pdf.

15. Joseph Stiglitz, "The Theory of Local Public Goods," in *The Economics of*

Public Services, eds. Martin Feldstein and Robert P. Inman (London: Palgrave McMillan, 1977), 274–333.

16. Chang-Tai Hsieh and Enrico Moretti, "Housing Constraints and Spatial Misallocation," *American Economic Journal: Macroeconomics* 11, no. 2 (2019): 1–39.

17. Ethan Elkind, *Railtown: The Fight for the Los Angeles Metro Rail and the Future of the City* (University of California Press, 2014).

18. Leah Brooks and Zach Liscow, "Infrastructure Costs," (working paper, 2019), http://dx.doi.org/10.2139/ssrn.3428675.

19. Chris Goodman, "Local Government Fragmentation: What Do We Know?" *State and Local Government Review* 51, no. 2 (2019): 134–144.

20. Jenny Schuetz, "Exclusive Communities Deepen Inequality in Every Metro Area," *Up Front* (blog), Brookings Institution, July 16, 2020, www.brookings.edu /blog/up-front/2020/07/16/exclusive-communities-deepen-inequality-in-every -metro-area/.

21. Chris Goodman, "The Fiscal Impacts of Urban Sprawl: Evidence from U.S. County Areas," *Public Budget and Finance* 39, no. 4 (2019): 3–27.

22. U.S. Census Bureau, "2018 American Community Survey 1-Year Estimates," Table B01003. Excludes unincorporated parts of counties.

23. City of San Marino, "Community Development Department," 2021, www .cityofsanmarino.org/government/departments/planning___building/index .php.

24. Myron Orfield, *Metropolitics: A Regional Agenda for Community and Stability* (Brookings Institution Press, 1997), www.brookings.edu/book/metropolitics/.

25. Federal Transit Administration, "Metropolitan Planning Organization (MPO): Overview," last updated March 11, 2019, www.transit.dot.gov/regulations -and-guidance/transportation-planning/metropolitan-planning-organization -mpo.

Chapter 8

1. Jenny Schuetz, "Democrats Hear the 'Yes In My Backyard' Message," *The Atlantic*, July 30, 2019, www.theatlantic.com/ideas/archive/2019/07/democrats -who-want-help-sky-high-rents/594787/.

2. Jo Becker, Sheryl Gay Stolberg, and Stephen Labaton, "Bush Drive for Home Ownership Fueled Housing Bubble," *New York Times*, December 21, 2008, www.ny times.com/2008/12/21/business/worldbusiness/21iht-admin.4.18853088.html; Office of the White House Press Secretary, "Making Homeownership More Accessible and Sustainable," The White House of President Barack Obama factsheet, 2015.

3. Emily Badger, "Renters Are Mad. Presidential Candidates Have Noticed," *New York Times*, April 23, 2019, www.nytimes.com/2019/04/23/upshot/2020-democrats -court-renters.html?searchResultPosition=1; Alissa Walker, "In Biden vs. Sanders Race, Two Differing Visions for Housing," Curbed, March 5, 2020, https://archive .curbed.com/2020/3/5/21165008/democratic-primary-joe-biden-bernie-sanders -housing.

4. Thomas Beaumont, "Does Joe Biden Want to 'Abolish the Suburbs?' No," *Chicago Tribune*, August 27, 2020, www.chicagotribune.com/election-2020/ct-joe -biden-abolish-the-suburbs-fact-check-20200827-3lwobgvu75ajdpodsoz32tb2sm -story.html.

5. Anna Fahey, "More Homes, All Shapes and Sizes, for All Our Neighbors," Sightline Institute, July 17, 2018, www.sightline.org/2018/07/17/neighbors/.

6. ADUs take on different forms and colloquial names across the country; examples include basement apartments and converted stand-alone garages or carriage houses, sometimes called "granny flats" or "in-law suites."

7. Henry Grabar, "Minneapolis Confronts Its History of Housing Segregation," *Slate*, December 7, 2018, https://slate.com/business/2018/12/minneapolis-single -family-zoning-housing-racism.html; Jenny Schuetz, "Minneapolis 2040: The Most Wonderful Plan of the Year," *The Avenue* (blog), Brookings Institution, December 12, 2018, www.brookings.edu/blog/the-avenue/2018/12/12/minneapolis -2040-the-most-wonderful-plan-of-the-year/.

8. Lauren Sommer, "Minneapolis Has a Bold Plan to Tackle Racial Inequity. Now It Has to Follow Through," NPR, June 18, 2020, www.npr.org/2020/06/18/877 460056/minneapolis-has-a-bold-plan-to-tackle-racial-inequity-now-it-has-to-fol low-throu.

9. Laurel Wamsley, "Oregon Legislature Votes to Essentially Ban Single-Family Zoning," NPR, July 1, 2019, www.npr.org/2019/07/01/737798440/oregon -legislature-votes-to-essentially-ban-single-family-zoning.

10. Oregon State Legislature, House of Representatives, "Relating to Housing; and Declaring an Emergency," House Bill 2001, 80th Oregon Legislative Assembly, introduced in House January 14, 2019.

11. Taylor Smiley Wolfe, Public remarks at Boston Foundation webinar, October 2020.

12. Conor Dougherty's *Golden Gates: Fighting for Housing in America* (Penguin Press, 2020) covers California's housing politics in great detail.

13. Laura Bliss, "The Political Battle Over California's Suburban Dream," Bloomberg CityLab, April 5, 2019, www.bloomberg.com/news/articles/2019-04-05 /the-suburbs-that-fear-california-s-housing-bill.

14. Sen. Scott Wiener, "Major Anti-Poverty and Environmental Justice Groups Endorse SB 50," California State Senate Democratic Caucus news release, 2020, https://sd11.senate.ca.gov/news/20200123-major-anti-poverty-and-environmen tal-justice-groups-endorse-sb-50; Liam Dillon and Taryn Luna, "California Bill to Dramatically Increase Homebuilding Fails for the Third Year in a Row," *Los Angeles Times*, January 30, 2020, www.latimes.com/california/story/2020-01-29/high -profile-california-housing-bill-to-allow-mid-rise-apartments-near-transit-falls -short; Housing Is a Human Right, "California Housing Justice and Tenant Groups Oppose Scott Wiener's SB 50," 2020, www.housinghumanright.org/california -housing-justice-and-tenant-groups-oppose-scott-wiener-sb-50/.

15. California Department of Housing and Community Development, "Accessory Dwelling Units (ADUs) and Junior Accessory Dwelling Units (JADUs)," California State Government research, www.hcd.ca.gov/policy-research/accessory dwellingunits.shtml; David Garcia, *Will Housing Finally Break Through in 2021? A California Legislative Preview*, UC Berkeley Terner Center for Housing Innovation report, 2021.

16. Executive Office of Housing and Economic Development, "Governor Baker Signs Economic Development Legislation," Massachusetts Governor's Press Office release, February 9, 2021, www.mass.gov/news/governor-baker-signs-economic -development-legislation-0.

17. Connecticut General Assembly, Senate, "An Act Concerning Zoning Authority, Certain Design Guidelines, Qualifications of Certain Land Use Officials and Certain Sewage Disposal Systems," Senate Bill 1024, introduced in the House March 10, 2021.

18. Alex Baca, "Virginia Won't Legalize Duplexes Statewide This Year, But the Urgency Remains," *Greater Greater Washington* (blog), 2020, https://ggwash .org/view/75803/virginia-wont-legalize-duplexes-statewide-this-year-but-the -urgency-remains.

19. Kriston Capps, "Nebraska's Battle Over Single-Family Homes Is Not Much of a Battle," Bloomberg CityLab, February 12, 2020; Brandon Fuller and Nolan Gray, "A Red-State Take on a YIMBY Housing Bill," Bloomberg CityLab, February 20, 2019.

20. Matt Levin, "San Diego's Mayor Explains Why He Became a 'YIMBY,'" *Cal Matters* (blog), 2019; Madeleine Carlisle, "Elizabeth Warren's Ambitious Fix for America's Housing Crisis," *The Atlantic*, September 25, 2018, www.theatlantic .com/politics/archive/2018/09/elizabeth-warrens-fix-americas-housing-crisis/ 571210/.

21. Vicki Been, Ingrid Ellen, and Katherine O'Regan, "Supply Skepticism:

Housing Supply and Affordability," *Housing Policy Debate* 29, no. 1 (2018): 25–40; Ingrid Gould Ellen, "Can Gentrification Be Inclusive?" Harvard University Joint Center for Housing Studies discussion paper, 2017.

22. Brian Asquith, Evan Mast, and Davin Reed, "Supply Shock versus Demand Shock: The Local Effects of New Housing in Low-Income Neighborhoods" (Upjohn Institute working paper, 2020); Kate Pennington, "Does Building New Housing Cause Displacement? The Supply and Demand Effects of Construction in San Francisco" (working paper, 2020), https://papers.ssrn.com/sol3/papers.cfm?abstract_id=3867764.

23. Yonah Freemark (2019) studied short-run outcomes from limited upzonings near selected transit stations in Chicago and found that housing prices rose while construction did not change. However, Chicago is not generally considered a supply-constrained market, nor was this a broad citywide policy change, so this paper has limited applicability to debates over proposed zoning reforms in California or other high-cost markets. Yonah Freemark, "Upzoning Chicago: Impacts of a Zoning Reform on Property Values and Housing Construction," *Urban Affairs Review* 56, no. 3 (2019): 758–789.

24. Dougherty, *Golden Gates: Fighting for Housing in America.*

25. Email communication with Alex Baca, policy director of Greater Greater Washington, March 24, 2021.

26. Jenny Schuetz, *Is Rent Control Making a Comeback?* Brookings Institution report, July 17, 2019, www.brookings.edu/research/is-rent-control-making-a-comeback/.

27. William G. Gale, "Chipping Away at the Mortgage Deduction," Brookings Institution op-ed., May 13, 2019, www.brookings.edu/opinions/chipping-away-at-the-mortgage-deduction/.

28. William A. Fischel, *The Homevoter Hypothesis: How Home Values Influence Local Government Taxation, School Finance, and Land-Use Policies* (Harvard University Press, 2001).

29. Ronald Ladell, Senior Vice President at AvalonBay Communities, Public remarks at Rutgers University webinar, February 2, 2021.

30. Lehn Benjamin, Julia Sass Rubin, and Sean Zielenbach, "Community Development Financial Institutions: Current Issues and Future Prospects," *Journal of Urban Affairs* 26, no. 2 (2004): 177–195.

31. Elle Reeve, "The US Already Had a Housing Crisis. Covid-19 Has Only Made It Worse," CNN Business, May 20, 2020, https://edition.cnn.com/2020/05/20/success/rent-housing-crisis-coronavirus-covid-19/index.html.

32. Mark Balldassare et al., "PPIC Statewide Survey: Californians and Their Government," Public Policy Institute of California report, March 2021, www

.ppic.org/publication/ppic-statewide-survey-californians-and-their-government
-march-2021/; UCLA Lewis Center for Regional Policy Studies, "Analysis of 2019
UCLA Luskin Quality of Life Index," https://newsroom.ucla.edu/releases/housing
-costs-ucla-quality-life-index-2019.

33. Douglas S. Massey et al., *Climbing Mount Laurel: The Struggle for Affordable
Housing and Social Mobility in an American Suburb* (Princeton University Press,
2013).

34. Ford Fessenden, "County Sued over Lack of Affordable Homes," *New York
Times*, February 4, 2007, www.nytimes.com/2007/02/04/nyregion/nyregionspe
cial2/04wemain.html.

35. Susie Steimle, "Sue the Suburbs: One Nonprofit's Plan to Solve the Housing
Crisis," CBS SF BayArea, September 30, 2019, https://sanfrancisco.cbslocal.com
/2019/09/30/sue-the-suburbs-one-nonprofits-plan-to-solve-the-housing-crisis/.

36. Christopher S. Elmendorf et al., "'I Would, If Only I Could': How Cities Can
Use California's Housing Element to Overcome Neighborhood Resistance to New
Housing," UCLA Lewis Center for Regional Policy Studies, December 14, 2020,
www.lewis.ucla.edu/research/overcoming-neighborhood-resistance/.

37. Office of Policy Development and Research, *Eliminating Regulatory Barriers to Affordable Housing: Federal, State, Local, and Tribal Opportunities*, U.S.
Department of Housing and Urban Development, Regulatory Barriers Clearinghouse report, 2021, www.huduser.gov/portal//portal/sites/default/files/pdf/
eliminating-regulatory-barriers-to-affordable-housing.pdf.

38. Carolin Schmidt, "Strong Tenant Protections and Tax Policy Support
Germany's Majority-Renter Housing Market," Brookings Institution essay, April
20, 2021, www.brookings.edu/essay/germany-rental-housing-markets/; Arthur
Acolin, "The Public Sector Plays an Important Role in Supporting French Renters,"
Brookings Institution essay, April 20, 2021, www.brookings.edu/essay/france
-rental-housing-markets/.

39. Lauren Lambie-Hanson, Wenli Li, and Michael Slonkosky, "Institutional
Investors and the U.S. Housing Recovery" (Federal Reserve Bank of Philadelphia
working paper, 2019); Elora Lee Raymond et al., "From Foreclosure to Eviction:
Housing Insecurity in Corporate-Owned Single-Family Rentals," *Cityscape* 20,
no. 3 (2018): 159–188.

40. Monica Klein, Twitter post, May 11, 2021, 8:17 a.m., https://twitter.com/
MonicaCKlein/status/1392091392290217984; Editorial Board, "Shaun Donovan
Mayoral Endorsement Interview," *New York Times*, May 10, 2021, www.nytimes
.com/2021/05/10/opinion/shaun-donovan-endorsement-interview.html.

41. Mark J. Perry, "Chart of the day . . . or century?" American Enterprise Institute, 2021, www.aei.org/carpe-diem/chart-of-the-day-or-century-5/.

42. Katherine Einstein, Joseph Ornstein, and Maxwell Palmer, "Who Represents the Renters?" (working paper, 2021), http://sites.bu.edu/kleinstein/files/2021/01/Homeowners.pdf.

43. U.S. Congress, Senate, "Yes In My Backyard Act," S.B. 1919, 116th Cong., 1st sess., introduced in the Senate on June 20, 2019.

44. U.S. Congress, Senate, "Housing Supply and Affordability Act," S.B. 5061, 116th Cong., 2nd sess., introduced in the Senate on December 17, 2020.

Index

Figures and tables are indicated by "f" and "t" following page numbers.